HUNTING AND SHOOTING WITH THE MODERN BOW

by Roger Maynard

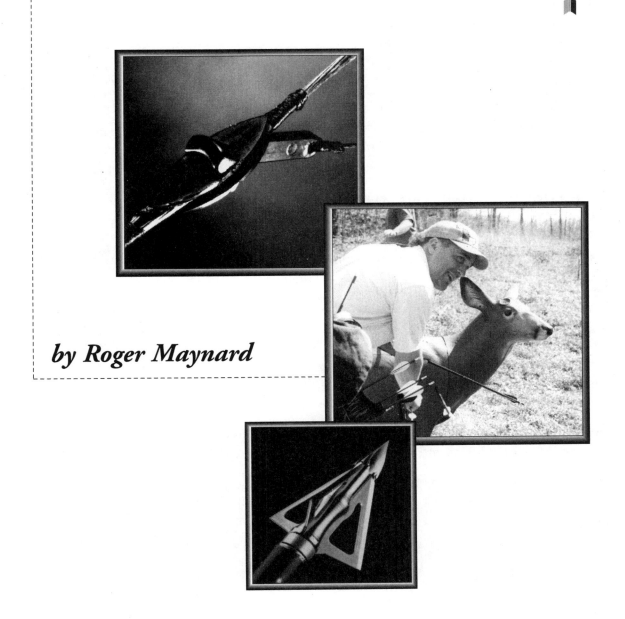

STOEGER PUBLISHING COMPANY

TITLE: *Hunting And Shooting With The Modern Bow*
EDITORIAL CONSULTANT: *William S. Jarrett*
PRODUCTION EDITOR: *David Johnston*
EDITORIAL ASSISTANT: *Michael Griffin*
COVER ART DESIGN: *Ray Wells*
BOOK DESIGN AND LAYOUT: *Lesley A. Notorangelo/DSS*
PROJECT MANAGER: *Dominick S. Sorrentino*
ELECTRONIC IMAGING: *Lesley A. Notorangelo/DSS*

Published by Stoeger Publishing Company
5 Mansard Court
Wayne, New Jersey 07470

ISBN: 0-88317-215-1
Library of Congress Catalog Card No.: 98-061495
Manufactured in the United States of America

Distributed to the book trade and to the sporting goods trade by Stoeger Industries, 5 Mansard Court, Wayne, New Jersey 07470

In Canada, distributed to the book trade and to the sporting goods trade by Stoeger Canada, Ltd., 1801 Wentworth Street, Unit 16, Whitby, Ontario L1N 8R6.

ACKNOWLEDGEMENTS & DEDICATION

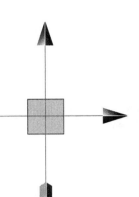

I want to express my deep gratitude and appreciation to the following people who helped me in preparing this work: Larry Guinn, Ollie Morgan and Randy Caple at *Hunter's Choice*; and Lewis Swan, Kevin Hays, Criss McNew and Dale Halbrook at *King's Outdoors*. Also: Mike Barnett, Bill Clements, Jimmy Jobe, Bob Johnson, Dr. James L. Smith, John White and to a multitude of manufactures and their representatives, including: Jim Fletcher (*Archery Aids*), Ray Browne (*BCI*), Sher Rosich (*Bohning*), John Anthone (*Great American Tool*), Rich Walton (*Hawk Associates*), Stanley Hips (*Hips Targets*), Ms. Kathy Velardi and Jess Edwards (*Hoyt-Easton*), Joel Maxfield (*Mathews Archery*), Dale Morrell (*Morrell Manufacturing*), Greg Martens (*Multiple Products Sales*), Mrs. Joe Platt (*Muzzy*), Andy Simo (*New Archery Products*), Mrs. Sandy Loomis, Dean Monticelli, and Jerry Fisher (*Oneida Eagle*), Keith Jabben (*Precision Designed Products*), Pete Shipley and Jim Jordan (*PSE*), Larry Faust (*Ultra Nock*), Dennis Phillips (*Walker Agency*), and John Zwickey (*Zwickey Archery*).

To my three sons—Roger W., Travis C., and Rayburn L.— for the pleasure they give me as I watch them training others in the archery and woodcraft skills they have come to know so well.

ABOUT THE AUTHOR

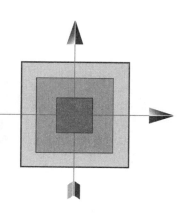

oger Maynard's lifelong passions have always been fishing and hunting, especially hunting with a bow. For nearly half a century he has been deeply involved in all aspects of archery, from the early beginnings of bowhunting in America to the present sophisticated state of the art.

During the Great Depression of the 1930s the Maynard family moved to Little Rock, where young Roger learned of a smallbore rifle match to be held nearby. The 13-year old lad tied his rifle across the handlebars of his bicycle and pedaled 14 miles to Camp Pike (now Camp Robinson), paying his entry fee with hard-saved cash. When the smoke cleared, the youngster had come within one point of winning the match.

During World War II Maynard served first as a small arms instructor, then in the Southwest Pacific with the Fifth Air Force, where he was wounded in action. After his discharge, he returned to the University of Arkansas to finish his studies and begin a career in civil engineering. Unable to overcome his crippling war wound, Maynard renewed an early interest in archery and bowhunting. Once the spark was rekindled, it never dimmed.

Like enthusiasts everywhere, serious bowhunters sought each other's company. Soon a group was formed, including such bowhunting pioneers as Ben Pearson, Dave Bosma, James L. Smith, Shelby Woodiel, Daniel Boone Bullock, Lewis Rush and Duane Holloway. This small group accounted for about 15 of the first 20 deer taken with bow and arrow in Arkansas. Bowhunting in those days was not easy. Seasons were short and there was opposition from many quarters to the use of the bow as a weapon for big game hunting, including gun hunters who considered bowhunting a threat to their sport. To counter these charges, the Arkansas Bowhunter's Association was formed with Roger Maynard as its first president.

Roger Maynard has been there and seen it all, from the longbow to the most advanced compound, and he has been successful with all of them. He has watched the shooting glove give way to the mechanical release and instinctive shooting replaced by the latest in bowsights. This book is the culmination of over five decades of learning, teaching and sharing the pleasures of archery and bowhunting.

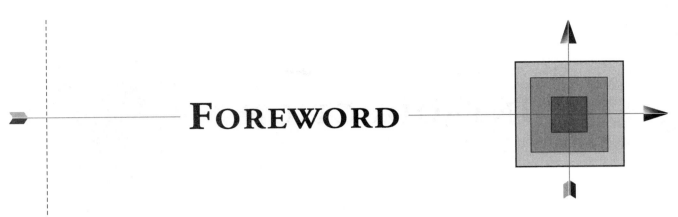

FOREWORD

i, Bowhunter! Somewhere in this book I have touched on most phases of archery all the way from Noah to you, the modern bowyer. There remain four basic approaches to producing today's compound bow. In preparing this book, I ordered a top-of-the-line model from each company specializing in making each of these concepts, or from those who produce a popular line bow that represents this concept. No effort has been made to affirm that one of these bows is better than another. Each one has performed admirably, and all are produced by top quality manufacturers. My goal is simply to help you achieve the level of accuracy these bows can provide.

There's a fifth bow involved as well—the recurve bow—which is the product of an amateur bowyer working out of a simple home workshop. The manufacture of recurves and longbows among serious amateurs is a hobby within a hobby, one that is growing in popularity all across the country. The basic steps are shown, along with several tips that will help readers start or add to their bow-crafting hobby. I also talk about arrows, bowstrings, woods cruising, and even how to become a leader in organized archery.

A final word of warning: The handling of chemicals, techniques and practices described in this book have proved injury-free for many years by the author, his sons, and many like-minded friends. Not having control over the actions of those who attempt what we have prescribed in this book, Stoeger Publishing Company and its sales agents, the author and his sons shall remain free from any form of legal action.

– Roger R. Maynard

INTRODUCTION

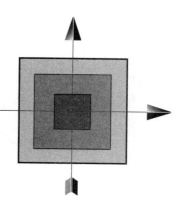

xpert bowhunter Roger Maynard follows up his highly successful *Advanced Bowhunting Guide* with an in-depth look at what it takes to be successful in the hunt for game using high-tech weapons based on designs that pre-date history. For instance, did you know that bows used by Napoleon Bonaparte's forces in the early 1850s bore a striking resemblance to the designs developed in the 1960s? Or that the predecessors to today's National Guard gathered on Medieval village greens each Sunday for archery practice? That the sons of Noah are credited with introducing archery to the northern Mediterranean area? Maynard explains it all in 37 heavily illustrated chapters, based on his knowledge and the advice from the army of bowhunters and bow makers he has met over his 30-plus years of hunting and tinkering.

Among the important subjects covered in Roger Maynard's new book are the following:

✦ *The History of Archery*
✦ *Marking Your Start in Archery*
✦ *The "PSE" Inferno*
✦ *Setup and Tuning*
✦ *Accuracy Aids*
✦ *Tracking Wounded Game*
✦ *Dressing Your Game*
✦ *Avoiding Injuries*
✦ *Game Management*
✦ *Spine and Paradox*
✦ *Making Arrows...and much more.*

TABLE OF CONTENTS

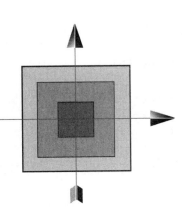

CHAPTER ONE

The History Of Archery

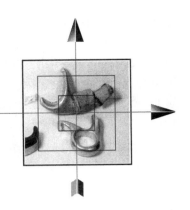

Prehistoric man had two problems: finding enough to eat and making sure he wasn't lunch for one of the mean creatures that roamed the earth. In this battle for survival against critters that were larger, stronger and quicker, early mankind learned to fashion weapons from whatever proved effective—be it rocks, clubs or fire—in defending itself against predators.

The first portable weapons were, most likely, pointed sticks, which evolved into pointed throwing sticks and, eventually, into longer and heavier spears. Those who look for clues to early tools and weapons in the Western Hemisphere have uncovered large flint points, such as those used on spears, ten times more frequently than they find the smaller points associated with arrows. This ten-to-one ratio, which exists from the Atlantic to the Pacific, indicates that a lot of stick or spear points existed for every point mounted on an arrow.

Actually, historians have failed to agree on the origin of the bow and arrow, although the biblical account of Noah indicates his sons brought this skill with them on the ark and proceeded to spread their knowledge. The Old Testament refers several times to archery as a characteristic skill of the ancient Hebrews, particularly the "Tribe of Benjamin." These were followers of the younger brother of Joseph, who settled northeast of the Mediterranean.

The Romans were particularly skilled with the bow and arrow, a significant factor in their military superiority. One of the Romans' tactics—a forerunner of the modern archery contest—was to shoot a brilliantly colored arrow high into the air so that it would fall in the midst of the enemy troops. For the Romans, the bright arrow served as a reference point. Within seconds of its landing, a mass of arrows would rain down from the sky. Modern archery retains this form of competition in what's known as "clout shooting."

Another archery skill developed by the Romans was "wand shooting," which included firing from 100 yards away at a flat-sided stake stuck in the ground . This practice honed the skills of archers who were trained to shoot at thin slits in castle walls during sieges. There is, after all, nothing like an arrow whistling across one's bedroom to dispel all thoughts of invincibility.

Archery certainly precedes the period of Roman dominance. In Greek mythology, for instance, Achilles is said to have died during the Trojan War after Paris had fired an arrow into Achilles' only unprotected area, his heel. It was a shot either of great skill or great luck. Near the beginning of the Middle Ages, Rome fell as even more skillful archers among the Goths, Huns and Vandals ended the long rule of the Romans. The Huns, led their king, Attila, were armed with short, horn-laminated bows and a quiver full of iron-tipped arrows. Attila, whose cavalry had become the most devastating in the world, died in 454 just as he was ready to invade Italy for a second time. Upon his death, his army scattered, leaving behind much of the recurve laminated bow technology along with examples of the Huns' beautiful, hammered iron-tipped arrows.

During the Middle Ages, the English became known as Europe's greatest archers, their exploits recounted in song and ballad. During the Renaissance, which began in the 14th century, European travelers found bows and arrows used in the Far East, the Americas, Central Africa and even in the Arctic regions. The materials used for these bows varied from time to time and place to place. The recurve bow was discovered in the Middle East and areas of the Far East, while the straight-ended longbow developed in Europe and the Americas. Surprisingly, the most advanced bows were found in areas where no native woods existed.

Howard Hill, one of the finest archers of his time (and the man responsible for sparking my interest in archery), wrote many books on the subject, one of which makes the first mention that I recall of a laminated bamboo bow. The skill of making an adhesive from animal horns was adapted to bow making, and thus the horn-laminated recurve bow was born. The glue has served mankind well; I still remember watching a skilled repairman use warmed glue to fix furniture back in the 1930s. The Huns are also believed to have left another device of modern archery: the slip ring release. The Chinese sometimes get credit for the development, but their release differs little from those of the earlier Huns and Mongols.

Archery continues to flourish in many areas of the world. In Africa, both the Pygmy and Wakamba tribes use bows and arrows, primarily for hunting. Since World War II, the dream of Olympic gold has rekindled the fire of archery in Japan, China, and North and South Korea, which all send teams to the competitions. And let's not overlook North America. I firmly believe more archers and bowhunters exist in the United States and Canada than the rest of the world combined. It was the Spanish, of course, who introduced horses to the Americas. Tales and films of the Old West typically depict an Indian riding alongside a herd of buffalo with his bow at full draw. In reality, the traditional Indian way of hunting buffalo was to stampede them over a cliff! Occasionally an Indian would shoot a buffalo with his bow, but he knew he'd have to blood-trail that buff if he expected to eat any of it. And for sure, he'd have to replace that arrow. Bowhunters have seen too many deer-sized critters ruin arrows when they were hit.I believe that when horses became available to the Indians, they opted for a heavy lance, a short ride and a well-directed hit, saving the squaws from having to search for the downed animals. The Indian was a good bowhunter, granted, but he was also smart and pragmatic enough to save his quiver of good arrows for prowling bears and enemy warriors.

One of the traditions of archery and bowhunting dates back to the end of the Civil War. A story is told of the Thompson brothers, two ex-Confederate soldiers who were left with nothing but empty stomachs and a skill for making archery equipment. Their homemade bow and arrows provided enough food to keep them alive until harvest. They wrote of their ordeal in a record that remains today. In California, a posse shot and killed one of the area's last group of wild Indians. One, named Ishi, escaped but was later captured and tossed into jail. Two men, Saxton Pope, a medical doctor, and Charles Young saved Ishi's life. In gratitude, he taught them his skills with the bow and arrow. Today, the Ishi Award is one of archery's highest honors.

Scared and bewildered, Ishi gradually learned the ways of the white man. With plenty of time, money and a burning desire for adventure, he, Pope and Young, who were by now close friends, bowhunted from Alaska, across North America and all the way to Africa, recording their hunts with a motion picture camera. After their return, the three men presented illustrated lectures about their travels. They were the inspiration for archer and film-maker Howard Hill and Fred Bear, founder of the famed archery company. Competitive archery in the United States began before World War II under the auspices of the National Target Association and with a big assist from the Boy Scouts of America. Hill toured the United States, giving archery

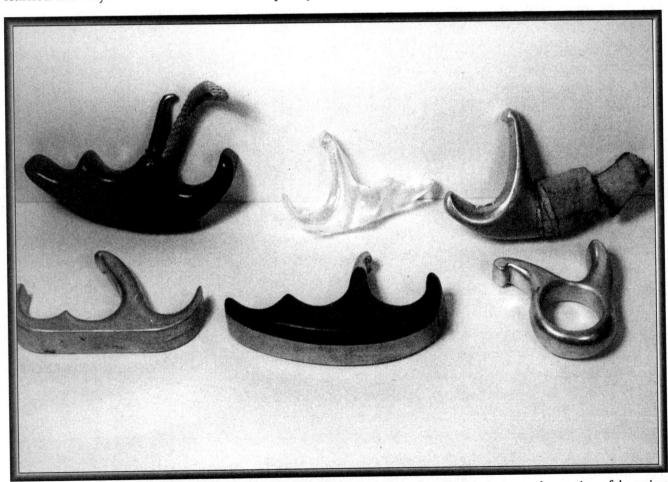

Attila's Huns probably introduced the slip-ring release techniques to the European archer. Shown are some modern versions of the ancient shooting aid.

exhibitions and making film documentaries. The passions for their sport, put on hold by World War II, was quickly rekindled among U.S. bowhunters at war's end. Hill's film of his hunt in Africa in the 1950s played in movie theaters across the nation. Former Boy Scouts dusted off merit badge skills, and suddenly bowhunting and tournament shooting became the rage. Archery's popularity has grown ever since.

Despite its horrors, World War II brought technological advances that continue to serve us. Among them is the chemistry that led to the development of fiberglass, epoxy adhesives and the polyester fiber bowstring, principally sold under the trade name Dacron. High-tech wood-working machinery produced precision-cut wooden bow laminates, while improved metallurgy turned the primitive aluminum arrow shaft into the finest arrows in the world. Plastic vanes guide many of our arrows today, but if I had to make that shot at Achilles' heel I'd choose an arrow fletched with feathers from the wings of a turkey. Mother Nature is not through yet!

In the 1930s, Dr. Claude J. Lapp created a compound bow. It shot well, but traditionalism reigned and he abandoned his efforts. Late in the 1960s, H.W. Allen designed and patented his version of the "compound." Traditionalists still ruled the Olympics and other international competitions, but the average bowhunter and field archer began complaining: "Bring on the compound. It outperforms the recurve." It was not an easy switch. When the compound bow first faced the finest recurves and longbows, many old timers chuckled at what they called "that contraption." I confess I was among them. The National Field Archery reluctantly accepted the compound, but the National Target Association still refused.

As compound bows kept showing up in the winners' circles at various archery competitions, however, some of the nation's top shooters began making the switch. Local archery shops were full of stories about H.W. Allen and how he and his associates were ignored by bow producers in their attempts to sell the manufacturing rights to the compound. But the compound bows kept winning, and suddenly the recurve bow was history. You couldn't give one away, never mind trying to sell one. Once the compound bow had arrived, men like Tom Jennings, Bob and Jim Carroll, Pete Shipley and several other small companies put their faith, hard work and scarce money into the compound.

Since then, the compound bow has undergone many design changes leading to four basic concepts of the compound bow:

◆ *The SOLO Cam Bow (by Matthew McPherson)*
◆ *The standard compound equipped with overdraw technologyfor increased speed (by Pete Shipley)*
◆ *The conventional two-wheel compound honed to perfection for accuracy and smoothness of draw (by Hoyt Bows)*
◆ *The unusual Oneida Eagle, which has the look of a recurve but with plenty of compound features.*

Meanwhile, reports of the demise of recurves and longbows were exaggerated. They simply went into hibernation in the 1970s and '80s, awakening in the '90s with the rebirth of traditional archery. Ironically, this "old archery" concept is now on the increase. Much of its success springs from the growing number of archers who "build their own." In Arkansas alone, more than 40 home bowyers are now creating their own bows. ▲

CHAPTER TWO

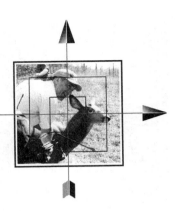

Making Your Start In Archery

 I overheard a young friend describe a recent visit to a local golf professional. He told in detail how the pro measured him for the correct club length and watched his every move as he learned the basics.

Compare that approach to that of many beginning archers. The neophyte typically buys the latest model of the bow that his buddy shoots, justifying its weight by rationalizing that he is 30 pounds heavier than his friend; besides, the bow has a 65 percent let-off. He compounds that mistake with two others: he expects to "work his way into the proper handling of the bow," and he gets his buddy to teach him to shoot. The problem is, his friend is trying to correct the errors he developed over three years of shooting.

Justin Callison likes good equipment too.

A good practice range makes archery more enjoyable and your skill increase.

Too many beginners believe that archery is a skill of strength only to discover that mind and body must work together to control the flight of the arrow. Here is a better way to begin:

STEP 1. *Find an archery shop with indoor shooting facilities and competent instructors.*

STEP 2. *Start with a used bow; an average adult male will likely be comfortable with a peak draw weight of between 40 and 50 pounds. Buying a used bow rather than a new one can save enough money to pay for six XX75 aluminum arrows and several lessons. Have the shop owner set the draw length that is best for you.*

STEP 3. *Select a simple pin sight and a string peep with a minimum opening of 1/8" diameter. Have the shop owner help you set your nocking point and string peep.*

STEP 4. *Buy a mechanical rope release with a wrist strap. Many archers consider this a tournament release, but I find it works well in hunting.*

STEP 5. *Once your bow is ready, select six XX75 aluminum arrows cut to length. Aluminum arrows are fine for beginners; wait until you are more experienced before moving to carbon.*

STEP 6. *Stick with indoor shooting until your form satisfies your coach. Once you shoot groups consistently, you are ready to move outside where distances can make you think you are trying to shoot across the Grand Canyon. Remember, the basics still apply: good holding, shoulder tension, aiming and squeezing the release trigger.*

About this time, your buddy will be miffed that you didn't let him teach you the art of archery. You can make amends in about three

Start them young.

months by coaching him out of his bad habits. This is also when you'll develop an itch for a heavier bow. Even though you have developed your archery muscles, you will do better with a draw of 60 pounds or less. Do a little research before you are suckered into the flat-trajectory speed craze. Consider the average distance of your game and plot the trajectories for a 60-pound bow and an 80-pound bow using a hunting-weight arrow. The results will be so close you will wonder what all the noise was about. Arrow placement is the name of the game; you will place that hunting arrow more accurately with a 60-pound rather than an 80-pound bow.

Three D tournament archers shoot all the draw weight they can handle using the lightest arrows the International Bow Hunting (IBO) rules permit. Consistent winners shoot at least several times a week, often every day. Heavy bow tournament archers work hard to move into the winner's circle, as do consistent champions in all sports. If you want to crack that circle, you have to work for it.

By now you are spending a lot of time shooting, and your enthusiasm could well infect one of your children who will want to join you on this adventure. He (or she) will want a bow, but you will have to decide when that time has come. Try this approach:

STEP 1. *Explain that to become expert in archery he must develop a "Master Eye." It's a discovery you will make together.*

STEP 2. *Stand about 10 feet away and have him point a finger at your nose. It is very important that he choose the finger; no fair prompting. One day he may line up a left-hand finger with the right eye; the* next day he may switch. It can take a month, but eventually he will settle on one finger and one eye. He has discovered his Master Eye and his bow hand as well. If he uses the right eye and a right finger, he should hold the bow in his left hand. I know it's confusing, but he will be known as a right-handed archer.

STEP 3. Before you buy him a bow, clearly state the restrictions on its use. Stress the safety rules and install a firm safe-shooting discipline in his mind.

STEP 4. The best equipment for a youngster consists of a simple recurve, an arm guard and a shooting tab. If your child is between 6 and 10, an inexpensive fiberglass recurve will serve him well. Several identical light-spined aluminum arrows will let you teach him the basics. Matched arrows are as important to the child's shooting as they are to yours. Whatever you do, don't shorten your damaged arrows and give them to the child. Accuracy is important to him, and he won't achieve it with cast-off equipment.

STEP 5. By the time the child reaches the age of 10, he will want equipment like yours. Several companies make small scale versions of adult equipment. If your child shows any interest in competitive archery, he deserves quality gear. Discipline yourself to be a knowledgeable and understanding coach, and you can turn him into a winner. ▲

A group of archers shooting a 3-D range.

CHAPTER THREE

Mathews Solo Cam Bow

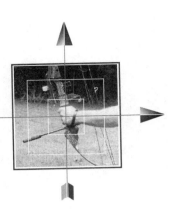

 s I said in the beginning, primitive man survived by becoming a skilled improviser, turning concepts into reality with the raw materials at hand. The late John D. Sanders once showed me a flat-limb laminated recurve bow. The limbs were backed and faced with rawhide, the pistol grip handle was built up with cork and the cut-out sight window looked like a 1996 design. The bow, built for Napoleon Bonaparte around 1812, had features that were 150 years ahead of their time.

The end of World War II marked the beginning of the trend away from natural products in archery toward man-made technologies. Ben Pearson and Fred Bear supplied North America with good mass-produced archery equipment. Earl Hoyt blended new materials into a very advanced recurve bow that dominated international competition. H.N. Allen patented the compound, and Tom Jennings, the Carroll Brothers and Pete Shipley turned the compound into a very popular bow.

Range testing the Mathews Ultra Light.

Shooting the Ultra Light with straight line nocking and a Fletchmatic wrist-supported release.

One of the bows selected for this book is the Mathews Solo Cam Ultra Light because it incorporates the one-cam power concept, which eliminates many of the two-cam bows' problems. Thanks to Mathews' engineering skills, the trend for several years has been toward shorter bows using less and less limb movement and more and more cam movement. The Mathews Solo Cam Ultra Light Bow was the answer to bowhunters' demand for a short bow; only 36 inches from axle to axle with a bare weight of only three and a half pounds — very short and very light. This very light net weight looked good on paper; even with the extra heft of accessories, it never reached the levels of other bows.

Doing what comes naturally to bow hunters, I started to pull on the bowstring and suddenly wondered if they had sent me a 70-pound draw weight rather than the 60 I had ordered. I asked my older son, Travis, to estimate the bow weight. We both guessed high; the scale showed the bow to be set on 60 pounds peak weight, dropping to 12 pounds minor.

The Solo Cam Ultra Light had been advertised at 80 percent let-off, and it produced it at 28-inch draw. Most other compounds attain peak let-off at 30-inch draw and produce a lower let-off weight at shorter draw lengths. It occurred to me that this bow must have a tremendous energy cam, if I plotted a draw-weight graph, it would show as much potential energy as any that I have ever drawn. My suspicions were confirmed by the chronograph and on the range.

Travis and I both have a 28-inch draw, and we set the Ultra Light up using a New Archer Products' Shoot-Thru rest. We installed a Check-It single-pin tournament sight that had been standard equipment on our hunting bows for many years.

The initial nock point was set 1/4 inch above 90 degrees to the bottom of the nock and secured with a Saunders clamp-on nock set. The new 1/4-inch Fineline string peep was secured in place. The steep string angle at full draw makes a large diameter string peep or an elongated string peep hole a necessity. We used a Fletchmatic rope release with a wrist strap and started shooting at 20 yards.

I have tried shooting fingers with a Wilson tab, but I much prefer a good mechanical release when shooting short-length bows with steep string angles. I recommend a 12-inch stabilizer for hunting and a longer one for targets or 3-D. For our first shootings, we used 2114-XX75 Easton aluminum arrows equipped with 125-grain Saunders field points and 125-grain Thunderheads with a four-inch helical feather fletch.

Travis urged me to "see what we can get out of this bow," so we installed a two-prong Merl's Shoot Thru rest with an overdraw. He picked Glen Turber's Nitro Stringer Tapered Carbonarrows fletched with 3-inch plastic Marco vanes. A PSE Mongoose sight was installed in order to qualify him for the "Bowhunter Release" class. Next he and Bob Johnston at Hillbilly Oscar's tuned the bow. They had a problem with the crossover bar on the sight, which was just a little short and jarred loose from the sight bar extension across to the multi-pin sight bracket. A machinist friend soon corrected the problem.

Checking three other makes of sights and two other makes of one-cam bows, we found the same problem with two of the brands of sights. Bowmakers have been very generous in providing sight window clearances to accommodate the multitude of overdraw arrow rests now available. To be safe, check this distance on any new model bow and sight combination while you are still in the archery shop.

Travis returned the bow to me, and I tried two types of straight-line nocking points — the Nock Lock II and the braided nylon cord. The chronograph detected no difference in velocity. With the Nock Lock II, the Fineline peep rubber tube is not needed as it is with the nylon rope. I used a Fletchunter hardnose release that I had converted to a wrist strap draw and a Gater Jaw release that holds above and below the arrow nock and had good results with both.

Choose your own release. Certainly a rope release that engages the string just under the arrow nock is a good, dependable setup, although I feel that either of the straight-line nocking points gives an advantage.

The conventional short energy-cam lightweight bow has a very definite recoil action. The solo cam concept is far gentler, providing a very smooth, jar-free bow. I recommend — and use — a short hunting stabilizer because I'm comfortable with it and it smoothes out my shot.

In short, solo-cam bows provide high performance in a small package, but they aren't for beginners. Serve your apprenticeship first, preferably starting with a used bow with a low draw weight at an indoor range under competent supervision. That's the foundation on which to build your future as an archer.

If most of my hunting were from a tree-stand or a blind, I would be very confident using aluminum arrows; the new Archery Shoot-Thru arrow rest; a Chek-It adjustable single-pin sight and a large diameter Fineline string peep; and a 12-inch hunting stabilizer. The type of nocking setup is a personal preference. Carry your arrows in a shoulder quiver or a detachable bow quiver.

If hunting in the more open country of the West — stalking, blind or tree-stand — choose a carbon shaft equipped with a glue-on 100-grain broadhead. I favor a Chek-It one-pin adjustable sight and a Fineline 1/4-inch string peep. Use a Merl's Shoothru rest with a short overdraw combined with a short hunting stabilizer. I recommend a straight-line nocking point and a hardnose release or the Gator Jaw system.

As for Mathews Solo Cam bows, I would use the Signature model for tournament and Western shooting because the longer bow gives you an advantage at longer distances. The Mathews line has several other bows, all short and fast-shooting. My son and I used the Ultra Light for most of the shooting and evaluation in this book, and I would welcome it in a tree-stand or blind. ▲

The Mathews Ultra Light showing a short hunting stabilizer, Merl's Shoot Thru Rest with overdraw, a wrist strap, and a Chek-it single pin sight.

CHAPTER FOUR

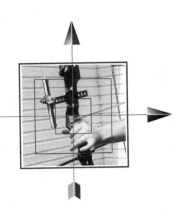

The Hoyt Legacy

 heck the bows used by long-time hunters and you'll find that many still prefer longer bows, even those who changed from fingers to a mechanical release. Oldtimers develop an eye for distance. If one says, "That stump is 38 yards," you'll find he's pretty close. The ability to judge distances will never disappear from bowhunting.

The tendency to stay with the longer compounds is a holdover from the days of the recurve. Most of us shot a 5-foot-6 bow; some would tolerate a 5-foot-4; and the daring would drop to 5-foot-2. The arrival of the recurve led to progressively shorter bows.

Eventually, I plan to give in to progress and take a deer with a Mathew Ultra Light just to see how this new technology treats bowhunters. I love to experiment, but come opening day, I'll start with the other extreme covered in this chapter - The Hoyt Legacy. The four bows discussed in this chapter are all fun to shoot; with the proper arrow, I can succeed with any of them.

Shooting the Hoyt Legacy

The Hoyt Legacy being checked by one of my sons for a hunting bow.

Being an oldtimer, I guess that it is natural that I chose the two longest bows of the four, the Hoyt Legacy and the Oneida Eagle X80. I feel comfortable with a longer bow, and I know how I want it to feel. The Legacy felt right when I checked it, both with fingers and a release.

Longer compounds can shoot a heavy hunting arrow with considerable authority, a quality that I like. Most of my game is taken with a thin-wall aluminum arrow because I like its flatter trajectory. When I hunt hogs, though, I want a thick-wall shaft because of the animal's tough hide and mass of muscle.

The Legacy is a little shorter (44-1/2 inches) than what I usually choose for a hunting bow, but this one is special because it was custom-built for me. You have a choice between a composite or a wood grip. I prefer composite for winter hunting. The limbs are 18-inch Hoyt Fastglass with 60 percent let-off energy cams, which draw very smoothly.

One of the first things I do when I climb a tree is find a place to hang my bow, quiver and a spot for a spare arrow near the area where I expect "Old Many Points" to present a target. Finally, I recheck my safety belt for comfort and ease of covering the area.

Many bowhunters impose a shooting range limit on themselves. This is a mark of good sportsmanship, and I commend them for it. They know how close they have to be to plant a killing arrow. Those who consistently fell game beyond past 30 yards qualify as skilled archers.

I know that I can take an animal well past 30 yards with the Hoyt Legacy, but much of this skill comes from accurate range estimation. My preferred shot at Old Many Points is broadside at 25 yards while he's looking away from me. I still take the shot at 35 yards with confidence. At 50 yards, I'll shoot only if I know the distance within a yard or two; I'll let him walk if the shot is not just right. The Legacy will give me top performance as long as I do my part.

I plan to set up the Legacy several ways at the next tournament. I will have a Golden Key Tournament Shoot-Thru arrow rest for the Arkansas Bowhunter 3-D fall shoot. The nocking point will be a straight line braided nylon using a Fletchunter hardnose release with a wrist strap. My arrow will probably be 4060 Beman Hunters with 100-grain glue-in field points with 2-1/2-inch or 3-inch Marco vanes.

When the fall bowhunter shoot is over, I'll change to a medium stiff springy rest. I'll either keep the nylon cord nocking point or change to an Ultra Nok II. My arrows will be 2013 XX75 with a 4-inch helical feather fletch and a 125-grain Thunderhead. Our foliage change usually peaks in late October; until this occurs and the leaves start falling, I'll shoot aluminum. After that, I'll change back to the Golden Key Tournament arrow rest and 4060 Beman Hunter arrow with a 100-grain Muzzy glue-on broadhead. I'll still stay with the 4-inch helical fletch. Sighting equipment for all of these setups will be a single-point Chek-It adjustable tournament sight with a standard Fineline string peep opened with a hand drill to 5/64 of an inch.

I'll stick with a 12-inch hunting stabilizer and a device manufactured by "The Game Tracker" called "Spare Finger". It mounts on the side of the bow and holds the arrow in place. As you start to draw, the device drops free of the arrow leaving the arrow on the arrow rest. The "Spare Finger" is standard equipment on hunting bows used by me and one of my sons and has never let us down.

The bowstring is Fast Flight, which, with normal care, will give a long, useful life. The new no-stretch, super-strength bowstrings add much to the performance of this well-engineered compound bow that is stable, forgiving and smooth-shooting. You can take the Legacy into the woods with great confidence. ▲

CHAPTER FIVE

The PSE Inferno

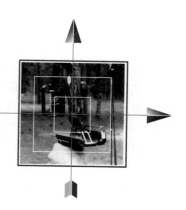

If anyone deserves the name "Mr. Overdraw," it is Peter Shipley. Pete did not invent the overdraw, but his technology made possible the greater arrow velocity that helps send many archers into the winner's circle. When 3-D shooting started rising in popularity, many turned to Pete Shipley for his overdraw knowledge and the products made at his Precision Shooting Equipment (PSE).

The overdraw arrow rest has become so popular that many see it as a standard modern touch on the traditional compound bow. The rest allows an additional sight window cutout and gives greater clearance for broadheads and fletching. The shorter distance between anchorpoint and arrow rest gives smaller diameter and lighter shafts the proper spine, which produces a higher velocity and a flatter trajectory. Because the arrow point is between you and your bowhand, it is never safe to shoot an overdraw rest without a properly designed guard.

My son Travis and I first met Pete Shipley around 1972 at the National Field Archery Tournament in Aurora, Illinois. Pete was displaying and competing with what was possibly one of PSE's first models. Today, Pete owns the company. He has earned a reputation as a builder of fine bows, and he is one of this country's best bowhunters. He made it easy to choose a bow that represents the blending of the overdraw arrowrest and the compound bow. I ordered a bow set to Shipley's specifications from Precision Shooting Equipment.

My Inferno model from PSE arrived with a 4-inch overdraw, a shoot-thru arrow rest, a PSE Mongoose sight and a bow quiver. The initial arrow matched to the bow was an XX75-2013 nocked 3/8 inches above 90 degrees. The arrow was offset 1/16 of an inch. A 12-inch Bomar stabilizer was selected for hunting and competition. Match this bow with good range estimation skills, and your game harvesting will improve greatly.

Travis chose the bow for his return to competitive archery. After a 20-year absence, he met the difference between field archery and 3-D shooting head-on and proceeded to master the techniques of this new form of archery.

He used an Arrow Dynamic tapered carbon shaft with a 3-inch plastic vane combined with 65-grain field points for the competition. He simply substituted the field point for the 65-grain Punch Cutter. It is an open-on-contract mechanical point that served as our field test for the model. The two skillet deer it took down came on classic broadside rib cage shots; both deer were taken within 65 yards. If all deer could be shot through the rib cage, the mechanical point would be a complete success; unfortunately, that's not the way it works. To my thinking, a dependable broadhead arrow must be capable of producing an entry and exit wound on any hit. Final judgment on these mechanical broadheads awaits more harvested deer.

The PSE Inferno showing the fiber optic PSE Mongoose sight. Combine this sight with a fine-line Sta-brite peep and you would have dependable accuracy under very poor light conditions. Also shown is the PSE Overdraw Shoot thru Arrowrest.

Let's go back to the 3-D setup. Travis and his friend, Bob Johnson, installed a set of Martin Speed Demons. They are small rubber buttons placed on a bow string with the use of a chronograph to determine the most efficient location. The buttons brought little improvement when installed on a simple roller cam bow. Put them on an Energy Cam Inferno, however, and you'll see an improvement of about 3 feet per second. Moving to a hard cam Browning added 5 feet per second. It seems that the more energy a cam produces, the better the buttons work. If you don't see increased arrow velocity while reducing the group size, I suggest that you re-examine the nock fit to your bow string serving.

Another common mistake is mixing arrow nocks. The vertical thickness of the nock groove can vary among brands. Nock length and taper diameter may vary without apparent problems, but changing the vertical thickness of the nock groove will open groupings. You can't mix nock sizes or brands without suffering the consequences.

Travis selected a 9/32nd Bjorn nock. The tapered shafts were cleaned with 91 percent isopropyl alcohol. The metal nock adapters were marked off and the shafts were dipped with two coats of Bohning white Fletch-Lac. The screw-in point inserts were installed with Devcon five-minute epoxy. The shafts were finished with 2 1/2-inch Marco vanes with just a minute amount of helix. The vanes were secured with Bohning Bond-Tite. Installing 65-grain screw-in field points gives the shafts a forward-of-center (FOC) balance-point reading of 11. A shaft this light with this balance point takes a very flat, stable trajectory.

The bow's draw weight ranged from a high of 65 pounds down to 54 pounds. After considerable shooting, Travis found he was most comfortable with 58 pounds. I'm glad that he settled on a medium-heavy draw weight. While he could handle a more heavy bow his choice of a more lighterweight reduced the possibility of permanent damage to his shoulder or elbow. When this damage occurs an archer can no longer hold or draw a bow. While you may think that reducing draw weight could let them continue shooting I am sorry to inform you that your bow shooting days are probably over. When this damage is done it is done and time will not effect a cure. Be smart and lower your draw weight while you can. ▲

Travis chronographing the PSE Inferno with Hunter's Choice Larry Guinn.

CHAPTER SIX

The Oneida Eagle Aero-Force X80

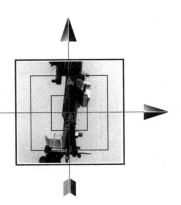

 recent 3-D shoot was winding down. As archers came in, their scores were posted and they enjoyed the camaraderie of a good shoot. An out-of-towner leaned a new Oneida Silver Eagle against the clubhouse patio wall; suddenly it was the center of attention as archers stopped to admire it.

The owner had equipped it with the best and latest accessories. The overdraw, fiberoptic bow sight and carbon shaft stabilizer were carefully chosen to complement its performance and attractive appearance. Owning the bow was a source of pride and an advantage in tournament competition.

The bow was an Aero-Force X80 trimmed in a very attractive camouflage pattern. It was equipped with a Tiger Tuff shoot-thru arrow rest and, later, with a Golden Key Medallion arrow rest for finger shooting, making it extremely versatile. The X80, equipped with a Perfect Draw control system, a choice of let-off modules and a Medallion arrow rest, hits me as a highly competitive finger bow. Why? Ask top notch finger shooters what holding helps produce the best results, and you'll find that many prefer a heavier shooting weight to help maintain proper shoulder tension and a cleaner release. The Oneida Eagle X80 gives you this choice of setup.

The setup for mechanical release included a Tiger Tuff shoot-thru rest and Saunders nock sets, a Chek-It Tournament sight and a standard Fineline string peep drilled out to a 9/64th diameter. A 12-inch stabilizer was installed for hunting and a 32-inch Easton stabilizer was used for 3-D tournaments.

The bow was equipped with a matching quick-detachable quiver, which I remove once I reach my stand and hang from a nearby location. Blaze orange and white are the predominate colors for my arrows. Moving these brilliant colors in a mounted bow quiver could attract attention whether your target is deer, bear or moose.

The recurve limb tips and limb structure make an Oneida Eagle bow extremely smooth drawing, and shooting is shock free. The X80 is an extremely fast bow, and while the longer roller cam bows handle heavier arrows well, the Oneida concept compares with the best.

Choice of arrows for the 35-55 pound X80 was the 2114-XX78 with a 4-inch helical fletch for hunting and a 2013-XX75 with a 3-inch Marco vane for 3-D using a release. The 2114-XX78 and Easton 6.1 PC shot well for fingers.

Adjusting the Oneida Eagle looks intimidating, just as it did on the first four-wheelers. A first-time experience with any mechanical device

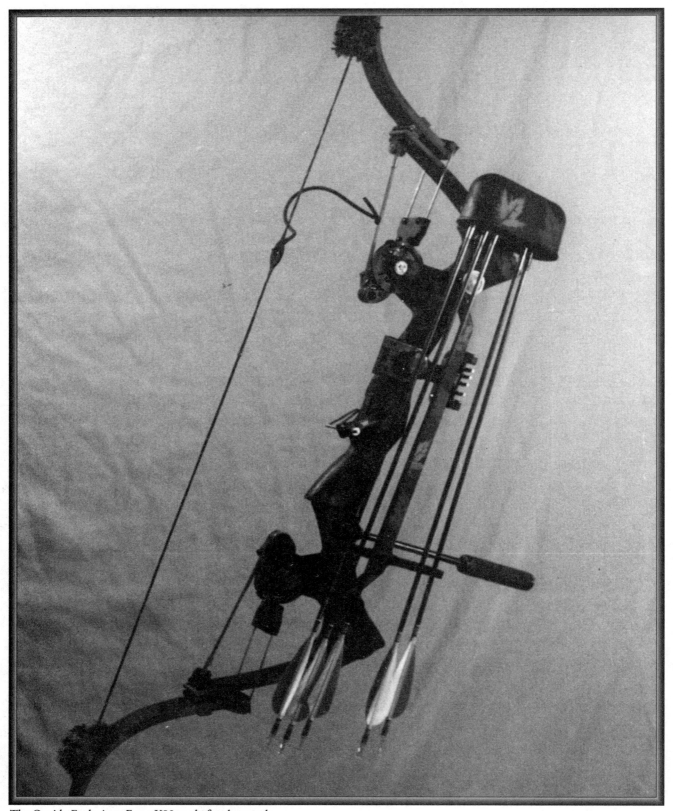

The Oneida Eagle Aero-Force X80 ready for the woods.

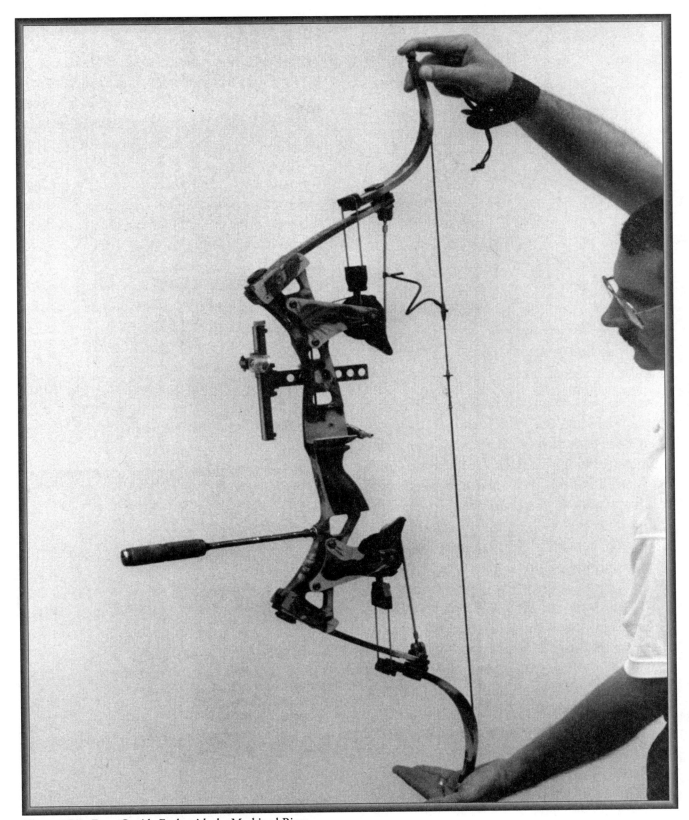

The new Lite-Force Oneida Eagle with the Machined Riser.

can be a rough. There are things to do and there are things you don't do, so identify these do's and don'ts:

- ✦ *Learn the difference between a socket head Allen screw and a button head Allen screw.*
- ✦ *Learn the location of these screws. The socket head is on the bottom cam of a right-hand bow and on the top cam of a left-hand bow.*
- ✦ *Always loosen the socket head screw before making a draw weight tiller adjustment or attempting to change a bow string.*
- ✦ *Always tighten the socket head screw before starting to draw the bow.*
- ✦ *Don't even think about loosening the button head screw for any reason. If you feel the screw needs to be loosened, return it to a dealer trained to adjust it.*

As you gain experience with the Eagle, you'll find it easier to use and friendlier than you imagined. It must be treated like the precision equipment that it is, and it will be a very trouble-free bow. Routine maintenance is needed on all compounds to assure proper performance. Follow the manufacturer's directions about lubrication; too little is better than too much. Because lubricants attract dust and other fine grain abrasives, apply it sparingly on flex points and roller shafts. Tri Flow and Rusty Duck are the two recommended lubricants. Tri Flow is available at most gun shops.

Watch your bow string. Many times during a 3-D shoot, a bow is leaned against a tree or bush while arrows are scored. Guess which part of the bow touches the ground the most? If you said bowstring, you are right. The bowstring collects abrasives at the bow tips and roller cams. Protect the bottom tip with a rubber or neoprene protector. Learn to hang or hold the roller cam bow up.

Familiarize yourself with the specific string your bow uses. The Aero-Force X80 uses an Omni-Flight bow string made by Oneida Eagle. When you consider how few bow strings you will use, sticking with the recommended Oneida Eagle won't add up to a major expense. A string made of the wrong material can cause major damage to the bow. Be practical and stay with the proper Oneida string, confident that the bow will perform as intended. This caution is no ruse to sell bow strings. It's just a fact that some bows cannot handle the new super-string, no-stretch materials.

The Oneida Eagle line of bow is the brainchild of John Islas. It is very versatile and performs like the top-line bow that it is. The Aero-Force X80 is equally at home on a formal target range, a 3-D range, in a tree stand or as an instinctive finger bow for hunters jumping and shooting rabbits along the edge of a southern swamp. No other bow draws and shoots like a recurve and still gives the performance of a compound. ▲

A bowhandle view of the new Lite-Force Machined Riser.

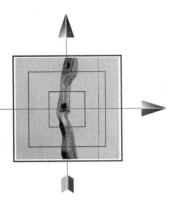

CHAPTER SEVEN

The Long Bow And The Recurve Bow

rom archery's beginnings to the perfection of the compound, the bow has existed in only two forms, each with infinite variations. It's like the wheel; from the simple concept comes a multitude of types. First came the longbow. Long or short, laminated or made of a single piece of wood, it survived in its basic form for thousands of years.

Second came the basic recurve. It, too, had many variations crafted from the extreme limits of Mongolia to the edge of the Bearing Straits. I once had the pleasure of examining a recurve built for Napoleon Bonaparte. To me, this bow was made into a 1996 design with materials from the early 1800s.

One variation of the recurve almost qualifies as a third basic form. The target bow used in international and Olympic competition was designed and built for York round shooting. Many modern archers think formal target archery is a snap, but the York is no snap. The competition requires shooting 30 arrows at distances of 90 meters, 70 meters and 50 meters. The bow is a recurve equipped with a tournament sight, a simple sight pin, but no sight level or string peep.

The world's first bow qualified for the name "longbow" regardless of its length. The shooting style was instinctive. The arrow rested on the top of the bow hand, which led to the expression, "shooting off your fist." Ben Pearson explained his uncanny ability to hit moving targets by saying, "Aim with your fist." Simple rests were devised originally to protect the hand from being rammed by a pointed fletch quill, but they also improved accuracy. Instinctive shooting often means canting the bow while sighting down the arrow that rests on a simple pad as close as possible to the fist formed by the bow hand.

When shooting a longbow, try locating the nock point a minimum of 1/8 inch above 90 degrees. Most of your shooting will be close range at moving targets, so choose thicker-walled aluminum shafts. Have a friend measure your draw length at full draw from your anchor point to 1 inch beyond the back of the bow. This extended arrow length protects the forefinger of your bow hand from being cut by the corner or edge of a broadhead as you reach full draw. Draw the arrow with your anchor finger above the arrow nock and your second and third fingers under the nock. Anchor at the corner of your mouth or where you feel comfortable. Wear an arm guard and shoot with either a glove or tab. This is archery in its purest form. Practice shooting at both moving and stationary targets or you will end up muttering, "If it runs by me, I can hit it, but if it stops, it's safe."

The next step in accuracy is space gap shooting; that is, estimating distances using the arrow tip as a sight pin. The space gap is the vertical distance between the arrow tip and the desired point of

The Sky Hawk by the master bower Earl Hoyt. Courtesy Hawk Assoc. and Sky Archery.

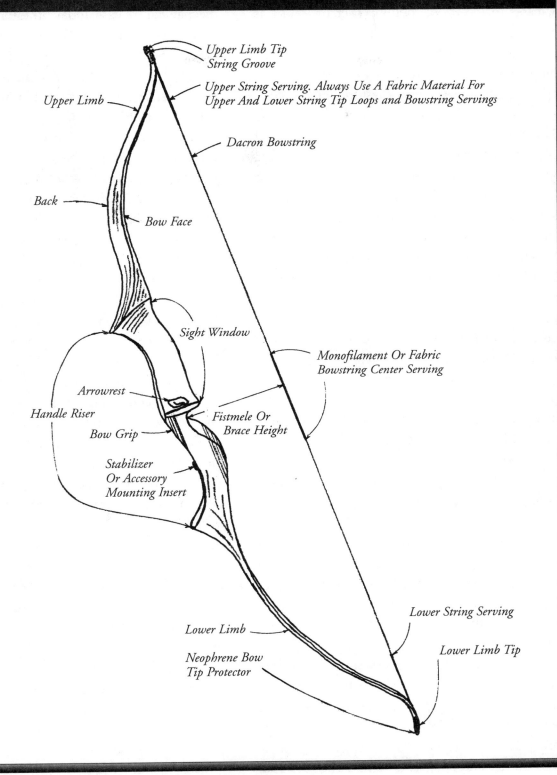

Upper Limb Tip
String Groove

Upper String Serving. Always Use A Fabric Material For
Upper And Lower String Tip Loops and Bowstring Servings

Upper Limb

Dacron Bowstring

Back

Bow Face

Sight Window

Monofilament Or Fabric
Bowstring Center Serving

Arrowrest

Handle Riser

Fistmele Or
Brace Height

Bow Grip

Stabilizer
Or Accessory
Mounting Insert

Lower String Serving

Lower Limb

Lower Limb Tip

Neophrene Bow
Tip Protector

impact, which is how "space gap" shooting got its name. The archer raises the arrow tip as the range increases to "dead on," holding over the target as the mental picture indicates a hit.

You can space gap with a longbow, recurve or a compound with the bow canted or vertical. Space gap aiming requires an arrow rest mounted slightly higher than your fist or sight window shelf. Many early arrow rests were made from a piece of a celluloid toothbrush handle and a piece of shoe tongue leather glued to the bow. A Hoyt Hunter or Hoyt Super Rest will suit space gap traditionalists using either a recurve or longbow. If you want to shoot a bare bow compound, try the Golden Key Medallion; or, if you want to hunt from a tree stand, try the Springy rest. Some archers use a form of aiming called "string walking." They place their draw fingers below the arrow nock, choosing whichever anchor point the distance indicates. You can bet that a good string walker is also a good estimator of distance. String walkers use the arrow tip as a sight pin. They raise the arrow tip as the range increases to "dead on" and then drop to a lower anchor point to keep from holding over the desired point of impact.

Precision archery originated at village green jousts outside some West European castle. It began as a series of marks on a longbow and has evolved into precision devices used at the Olympic course in Atlanta and at the traditional archery courses spreading across the United States. Technological advances turned sighting equipment into precision instruments that worked well with the new compound bow.

The plastics available to bowyers after World War II made possible the development of a practical flat-limbed recurve, a practical sight window and the Dacron brand of polyester bow string. Also from these plastics came the string peep, a super-light kisser button and adjustable sights. The stabilizer first made its appearance on a highly developed target bow as did the modern slip ring and mechanical release. Today, traditionalist archers shoot longbows and recurves and, if the rules permit, they will use the latest sighting equipment.

Arrows and fletching determine the choice of arrow rest. For a conventional 120-degree feather fletch rest, choose a Hoyt Super glue-on for ease of installation and good performance. If your sight window is cut deep enough for an adjustable rest, you might consider a 5/16th-inch, 24-threaded brass bushing. An older archery shop may still have this bushing in stock or know how to get one. Installing this bushing opens a wide choice of rests while allowing an in-and-out adjustment.

If I were to shoot fingers and plastic vanes, my first choice would be the Golden Key Medallion. This rest was designed for a metal handle riser, but it can be adapted to some wooden risers. It is a flipper-plunger rest, so I would use the plunger as an in-out adjustment with very light pressure for both plunger and flipper. Keep the plunger clean and free of lubrication.

Finger shooters should nock a little high to help clear the flipper rest. Avoid the shoot-thru rests unless you plan to use a release. A finger release is simply too erratic to provide dependable vane clearance. Make sure that you use a "Y" configuration for vanes.

The stabilizer helps reduce shooting-holding torque on any bow. The fistmele is the distance from a bow string to the bow handle. Your bow may have a pistol grip or a straight handle, so always measure from the same location.

Shortening the bow string increases the height of the fistmele, which quiets the sound of the bow and reduces bow recoil. It can also slow the bow cast by a small amount. Lengthening the string produces more sound and bow recoil and makes for a slightly faster bow. ▲

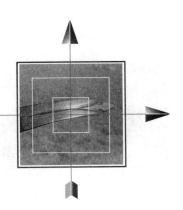

CHAPTER EIGHT

Jimmy Jobe's Recurve

 Mother Nature has a way of dealing with bowhunters by making them occasionally mow a lawn. While attending to this hot and overdue project, I was interrupted by the approach of a stranger, who wasted no time getting to the point:

"Mr. Maynard, I'm Jimmy Jobe. Can you show me how to build a recurve bow?"

I told him that construction of a laminated bow is very involved, requires considerable skill and access to woodworking equipment. I said I had seen a fiberglass laminated bow built, but that I not tried it because I had neither the place nor equipment to make a quality bow.

Jimmy said he was a cabinetmaker, that he had a well-equipped shop at home and, with a little help from me, he thought that he could make a good bow.

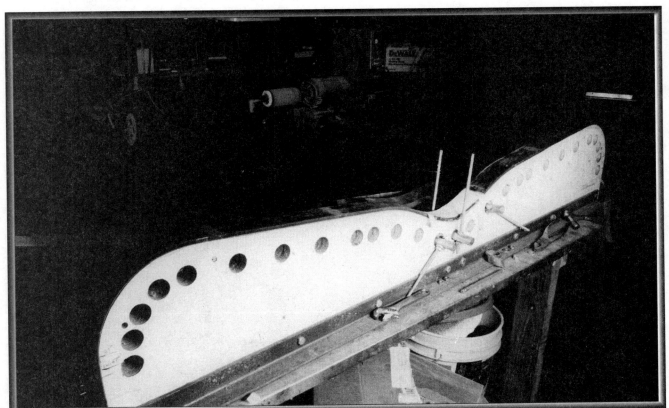

Jimmy's Bow Press

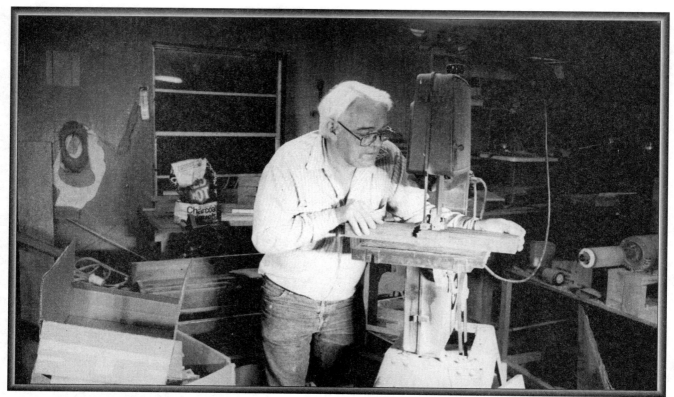

Rough Shaping the Handle Riser

Squaring each side of the Handle Riser

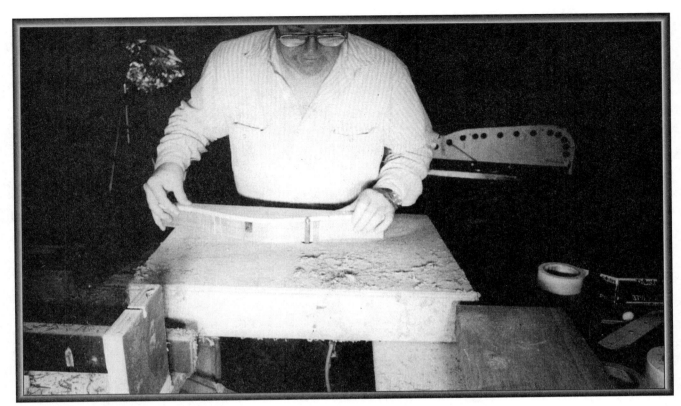

Rough trimming the limbs to the templates

Placing the bowparts in the press

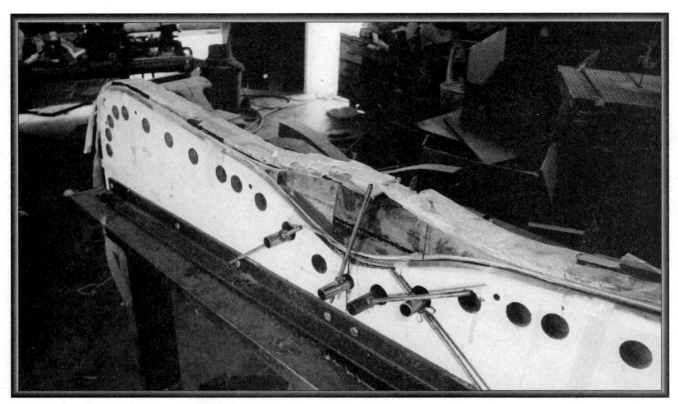

The "glued up" bow ready to leave the press

The rough bow being inspected

The sight window and tips are checked ror alignment

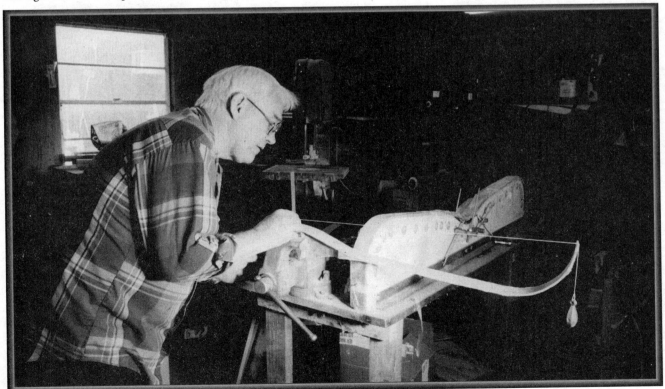

The sight window and arrow shelf are touched up

At this point, I found our conversation far more enjoyable than cutting grass, so we headed to my small shop. Jimmy examined my collection of recurves while I explained how the laminated limbs were "glued up" in a form that served as a mold and a press. If my memory is correct, we hunted up the address of Old Mastercrafters and Gordon Glass. At this point, Jimmy headed home for what I assumed was some deep meditation about his latest project.

After he left, reality sent me back to the lawnmower, and I mentally wished my new acquaintance the best of luck, although in the deeper recesses of my mind I suspected I would never see a "Jobe recurve." Two or three months passed when a telephone caller told me that in a few minutes I would hold and feast my eyes on the first example of Jimmy's craftsmanship.

His bow did indeed reflect the efforts of someone who took great pride in his work. It was equipped with a conventional string, but Jimmy wanted a "Flemish twist," and asked me to teach him how to make it.

Over the next few years, I talked with Jimmy several times, and each time he told me he planned to improve his next bow. During that period, a "Traditionalist Association" was formed in Arkansas, and Jimmy's bows frequently showed up in the winner's circle. Their beauty and performance gave him the reputation of a top hobby bowyer.

Jimmy's success and the steady growth of traditional archery in Arkansas give me an increased respect for bowhunting sportsmen in the United States and Canada. Arkansas has about 40 hobby-bowyers, and they say their hobby is growing in popularity across North

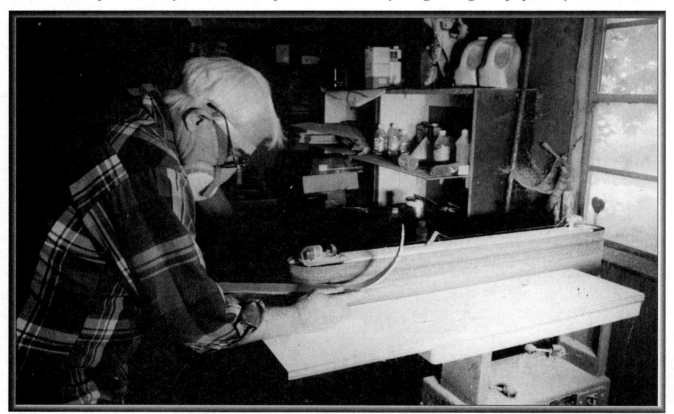

The bow limbs are sanded to template. Note mask.

Recurve Bow Ready For Gluing In A Bow Press

1. *Dry run with all parts to insure exact fit.*
2. *Epoxy coat all parts start pressure at riser.*
3. *Cure unit 130-140 degrees four hours.*
4. *Sand to remove excess epoxy* ***Use Mask.***
5. *Apply new alignment marks using string.*
6. *Install tip laminates.*
7. *Shape limbs to template.*
8. *Cut string grooves using long string.*
9. *Cut arrowshelf and sight window.*
10. *Final sand and apply finish.*

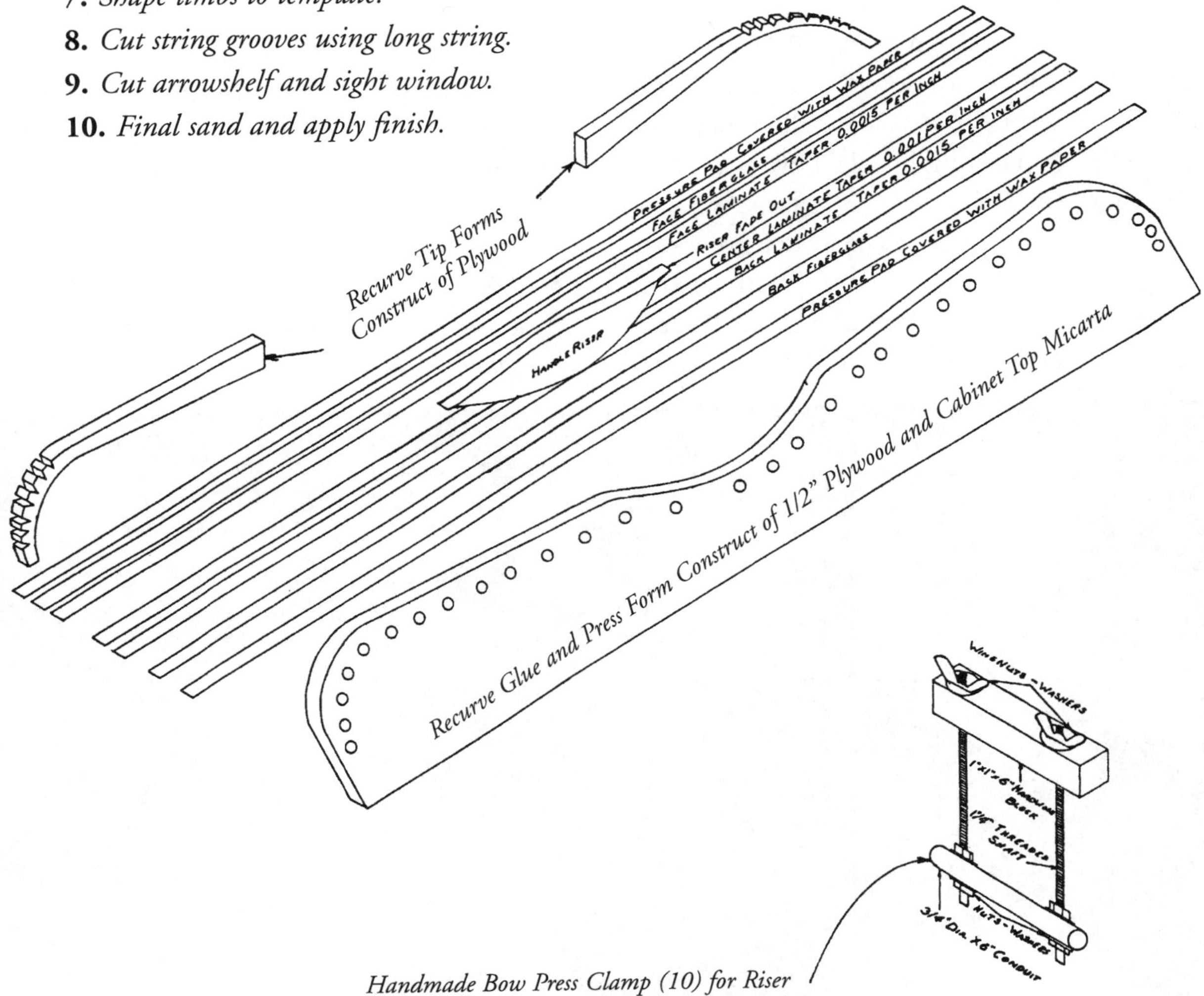

Recurve Tip Forms
Construct of Plywood
PRESSURE PAD COVERED WITH WAX PAPER
FACE FIBERGLASS
FACE LAMINATE TAPER 0.0015 PER INCH
RISER FADE OUT
CENTER LAMINATE TAPER 0.001 PER INCH
BACK LAMINATE TAPER 0.0015 PER INCH
BACK FIBERGLASS
PRESSURE PAD COVERED WITH WAX PAPER
HANDLE RISER
Recurve Glue and Press Form Construct of 1/2" Plywood and Cabinet Top Micarta
WING NUTS - WASHERS
1"x1"x6" HARDWOOD BLOCK
1/4" THREADED SHAFT
NUTS - WASHERS
3/4" DIA. X6" CONDUIT

Handmade Bow Press Clamp (10) for Riser Area. Use Conventional "C" Clamps elsewhere.

America. Their claim is supported by the number of advertisements placed by hobbyist/manufacturers in archery magazines. The demand grows steadily for custom-built recurves and longbows. Another surprise is the number of advertisements from bowyers offering to send instructions in their craft.

During subsequent interviews with Jimmy, he described two things that persuaded me he is a man who can think and act on his own. First, he copied the limbs of an old favorite bow and, second, he modified the handle riser on an old Super Diablo. By duplicating the old favorite, he mastered the basics of bow construction; its completion allowing him to compare the new with the old. Duplicating an old bow is a good idea for any aspiring bowyer; it saves time on design and gives an insight into bow construction.

Jake Mulliken, a true master listed in the Traditional Bowyers of America, helped Jimmy on his way to success. Jimmy's endless questions

to Jake, blended with his personal experience, produced these suggestions (remember, they are only suggestions — only you can produce the bow designed in your mind). Jimmy talked to many archers and so will you. Some of their advice you'll follow while ignoring others. These tips and suggestions are offered to make your bow-making more successful:

◆ *Get an Old Mastercrafters catalog. The company has been selling bow-building products for many years and has it all. It supplies individuals and large manufacturers, and its products are compatible with bow construction.*

◆ *Check your tools and make sure you have everything needed for the job. That includes furniture clamps and many sheets of sandpaper in degrees of coarseness, all the way to 600 wet or dry. I assume that you have the usual woodworking equipment.*

◆ *Make your first gluing form from the simple sketch in this chapter. I strongly recommend making a reproduction of an old favorite bow.*

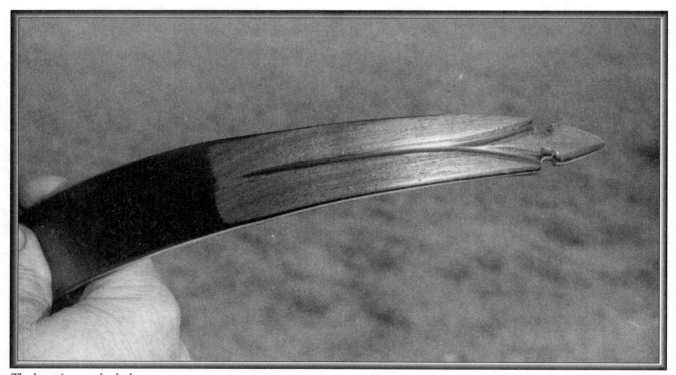

The bow tips are checked.

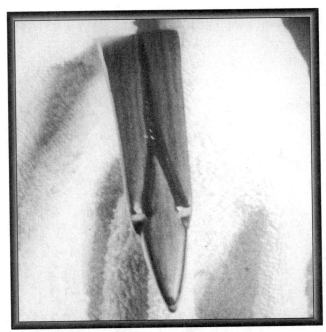

The bowstring and string grooves are checked

- If the temperature in your shop fluctuates because of the weather, consider making a simple curing oven. Jimmy uses four household light bulbs to maintain a constant temperature. Epoxy generates heat as it cures, so the more normal the level of internal oven heat the better the adhesion. Internal oven temperatures above 90 degrees are ideal. Avoid hot spots in the oven. It is important to put the bow and the mold in the oven immediately after gluing and clamping. Keep the curing bow in the oven for the time recommended by the epoxy makers. Curing the epoxy at a constant temperature as close as possible to normal produces the best adhesion. Avoid the super-fast epoxies.

- List each step as you build your first bow, and continue the practice with each additional bow. These simple listings can prove to be a valuable resource.

- Time spent drawing bow limb width and handle riser design saves time and expensive hardwoods. A roll of tracing paper from a blueprint company may seem expensive, but it will save time, material and your disposition. It will also provide patterns for future reference.

- Coat the molding surfaces and clamps with Johnson's paste wax to keep the epoxy from sticking. When you remove the bow from the mold, a simple wipe of lacquer thinner will remove any wax. Coating the mold with wax prevents a time-consuming refinish job should you decide to reuse the mold.

- Lay the wooden components on the fiberglass portions of the bow. The better the components fit, the better the bow and the faster you can start gluing and clamping. Remember, you will be working against time as the epoxy sets up.

- Cover the mold with wax paper and put a 1/4-inch pressure pad over the paper. Now is the time to recheck your fiberglass, limb laminates and handle riser fit. It's your last opportunity for any final adjustments.

- Measure the epoxy and hardening agents to the maker's specifications. Line a shallow plate with heavy aluminum foil to dissipate the heat from the chemical reaction as the epoxy and hardener are blended. A throat spatula is a good tool for

The string grooves are finished with a small round file.

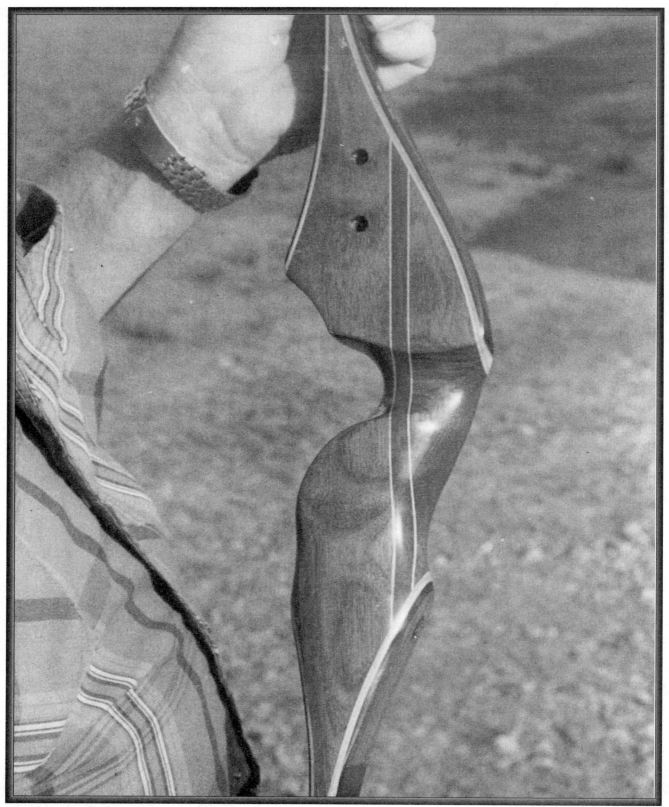

The bow ready to receive sight mount bushings

blending the components using a slow, mashing-stirring motion. Slow action keeps air bubbles to a minimum. Apply the mixed epoxy with a 3/4-inch stiff bristle brush. If you notice air bubbles, work them out with the brush. Your goal is a thin, bubble-free application.

If the bow component fit is good, gluing should proceed reasonably fast; start clamping at the bow handle and proceed toward the tips. Well-fitting, curved clamping blocks can reduce tip area problems to a minimum. If everything clamps flush with just a little effort, wipe the sweat from your brow, head for the fridge and pop the cap on a long cold one. You've earned it.

✦ *After the designated curing time, let the unit cool overnight before removing the bow from the mold. Use the paper tracings to transfer a center line and limb shape outline to the bow. Finish cutting the limb shape and glue on the pre-shaped limb tips. The tip pieces should have a flat side so they can be glued on with a minimum of clamp pressure. Let them set overnight.*

✦ *To prove this pudding, put a string on the bow and check its alignment with the drawn center line. Some adjustment can be made by a slight modification of the string grooves with a small round file. Don't be alarmed: slight bow adjustment is a normal step in bow making. Looking from the belly-string side of the bow, use the file on a grove displaying a limb twist. Once you've noted signs of a correction, finish lining up the bow. With a friend standing behind you, take a deep breath and draw your bow for the first time. If the tips line up at full draw, let out your breath. You are home free!*

✦ *You now have a roughed-out, aligned bow. Use the center line to finish out the edges of the limbs,*

Robert McDonald makes the test shooting

sight window, arrow shelf and handle. A word of caution: leave plenty of wood in the grip area. For now, avoid the slim and trim handle look. We do not want a two-piece bow at this time.

- ✦ Finish sanding the exposed wood using rough grit to start and progressing to lighter paper as needed.
  - – Drill and install the arrow rest.
  - – Apply finish to the bow.
  - – Use two coats on the edges of the limb laminations and bow tips.
  - – Don't fill the string grooves--a limb twist could start from just a thin coat of finish.
  - – To counter heavy wear, apply six or seven coats of finish on the handle.
- ✦ Install hardware and nocking point and check the draw weight. Choose an arrow that should match the bow, let it fly, then start on your next model. You and I both know it's already in the planning stage.

Jimmy Jobe still makes really good bows and continues to plan improvements for his next model. Another of his characteristics that I admire is his eagerness to pass on his new skills to other beginning hobby bowyers. ▲

JOBE'S PREFERRED MATERIALS

SMOOTH-ON-EPOXY – *Use for fiberglass, laminates, handle risers and bow tips.*

FULLAPLAS – *A clear finish for beauty and durability.*

LAMINATES – *Jimmy uses three tapered laminates. He feels that multiple laminates limit the damage should an epoxy void occur.*

FIBERGLASS – *Jimmy's choice of bow glass is the choice of bowyers everywhere: Gordon Glass.*

PRESSURE PAD – *An aid used to help apply even pressure while gluing wood surfaces.*

A bowhunter looking forward to bow season

CHAPTER NINE

Setup And Tuning

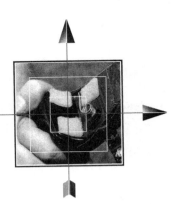

Setting up and tuning a new compound should not be an intimidating experience. Your purchase of a bow from a dealer probably means that some of these checks have been made. As you unpack the bow, the first thing to do is find the owner's manual and read it carefully before drawing the bow.

Next, make the following checks:

1. Measure the tiller height at each end of the handle riser. Place a ruler on the bow limb so that it just touches the end of the handle riser and forms a 90-degree angle with the bow string. At this stage, equal tiller measurements are desirable. Correct tiller heights by using the weight adjustment screws. Tightening the screws

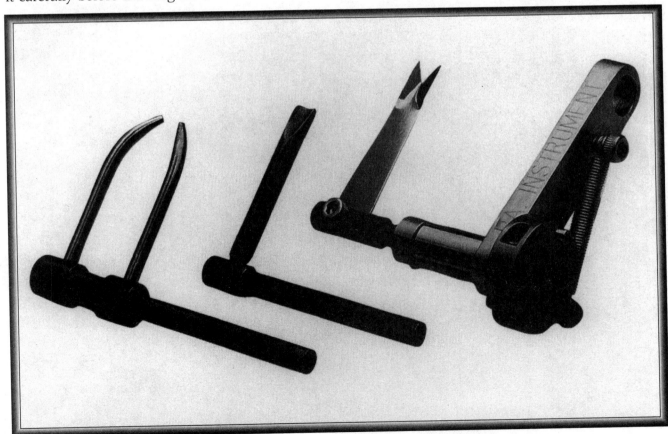

The stainless steel Pro-Rest shown with three launcher arms. Courtesy Pennsylvania Instruments Corp.

will shorten the tiller height and loosening them will increase it.

2. *Lean the bow in a vertical position against a table edge. Step back several feet and sight-align the bow string with the bow limbs. The center line of the limbs should parallel the edge of the sight window. If the bow is not in alignment, suspect damage to the shipping carton. If it is slight and the bow is out of alignment, the handle is probably bent. Neither problem can be corrected locally, so notify the shipping company.*

Another source of misalignment is heat from sunlight while in storage or in transit. The use of fast-setting epoxies by some small, inexperienced bowmakers in an effort to speed production can cause this problem. Some fast-setting epoxies can start softening at 155

Using the Pacesetter Targetmaster Shoot Thru Arrowrest by Golden Key Futura, Inc.

Fletching can be damaged by a overdraw shoot thru rest and hunting length fletching.

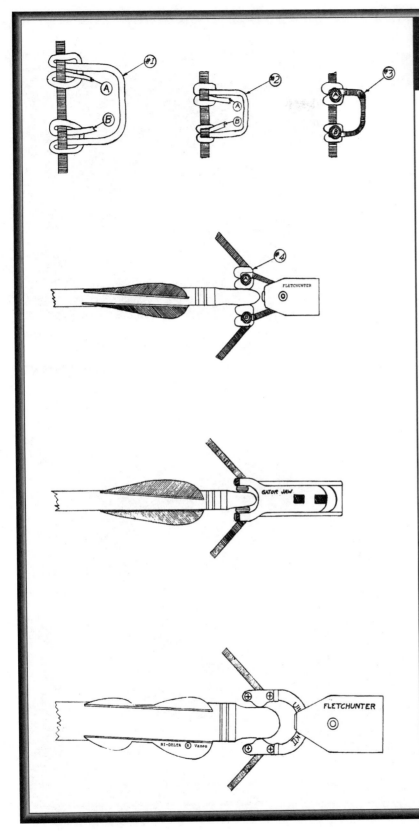

STRAIGHT LINE NOCKING POINTS

1. Shown in a open position to show how the knot is formed. Use 1/8" braided nylon release cord available at your archery shop. Note cord ends **A** and **B**. They should face your bow arm.

2. The stringloop knots are shown tightened down for positioning. Use a good snapnock on your arrows to make a loose bowstring fit leaving you dependent on the snap portion of the nock to draw the arrow. Do not attempt to draw and arrow until Step #3 is complete.

3. Heat swell **A** and **B** to make the knots hold. Stick cord ends **A** and **B** through small holes in heavy aluminum foil to protect bowstring and loopknots from the heat as they are swelled. A clean tipped soldering iron does an excellent job. Make sure that the arrownock is fairly loose or the arrow may jump off the arrowrest just as let-off occurs. Serve string loop with small diameter monofilament keeping maximum diameter smaller than the groove in a hard-nose release. The monofilament serving is optional, it is a handserved item and I would recommend it.

4. Shows the stringloop nocking point with arrow and hardnose release at fulldraw. Note a minimum 1/32" clearance gap between the end of the arrownock and hardnose release. The loop should be as short as possible to avoid disturbance of an old familiar anchor point. The stringloop places your release directly behind the arrow providing a smoother application of power as the arrow is released and the rear of the arrow approaches the arrowrest. The stringloop definitely makes tuning easier for the short axle to axle length bows. Many tournament archers feel that it provides a smoother set-up for longer bows.

The Gator Jaw hardnose release locks on to the bowstring above and below the arrownock is shown with the bowstring built up with dental floss to allow for nock thickness variation.

The Ultra-Nock II – A machined aluminum device that clamps on your bowstring that provides a much smoother arrow launch. The contact point of your hardnose release is directly behind and inline with your arrow. This nocking point provides much easier arrowflight tuning. The 32 grain weight increase will reduce arrowcast from 2 to 4 feet per second when using hunting weight arrows which should be no problem within reasonable hunting ranges. This nock device solves a lot of stringpeep problems.

degrees. Heat damage can be very obvious or it can be well concealed, leading to limb failure shortly after the bow is placed in service. The bowmaker's warranty is your best protection.

3. *If an object is stuck in the string of a new bow, don't pull it out. It divides the string into equal parts to help install the string peep.*

4. *Install the arrow rest. There is a 5/16 inch-24 thread bolt hole through the handle riser for this purpose. Adjust the rest up or down until the center of the bolt end and the major diameter of the arrow shaft match.*

5. *Establish the nock point by going 3/8 inch above 90 degrees. Use a screw-it bow square made by BPE Inc. (it works well with a shoot-thru arrow rest). Screw the projecting 8-32 screw into the arrow insert or outsert, and clamp the square on the string,*

The **Pro-Model Universal Crimping** tool by **Tru Fire** clamps your brass nocking rings then removes them if you desire.

Dale Morrell's Eternity Target handles my target and field points while Stanley Hips' Replaceable Core Target stops my broadheads.

MAKING YOUR NOCK HEIGHT SETTING

STEP No. 1

Make sure that arrowshaft spine is within spine chart range. Favor slightly stiff and heavier arrow weights until you gain shooting experience.

STEP No. 2

Set nock height with a bow square. 3/8" to 1/2" maybe slightly high for a release and about right for a finger shooter.

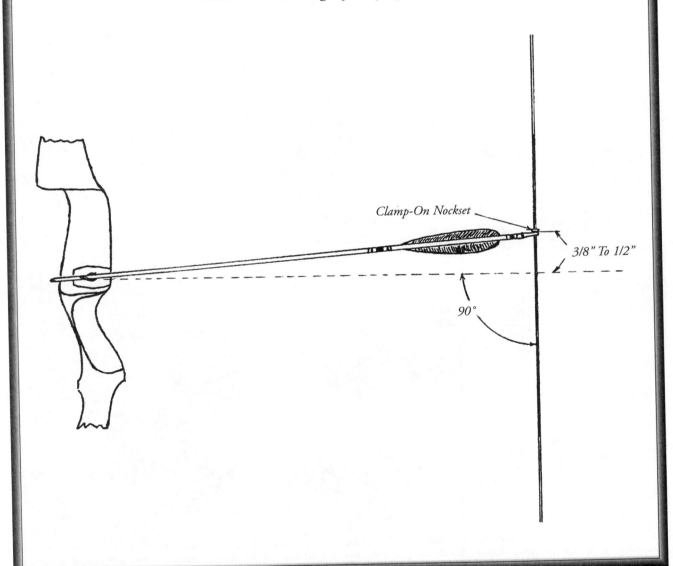

Clamp-On Nockset

3/8" To 1/2"

90°

laying the reversed arrow on the rest. Measure up 3/8-inch to locate the bottom of a Saunders clamp-on nock set. Clamp it on with medium pressure so the nock height an be adjusted up or down by twisting it when shooting begins.

6. Make a temporary installation for the kisser button. Use medium pressure on the two metal clamps provided.

7. As a temporary installation, insert a smooth pointed object at the factory-installed string divider used for expanding the string, then insert the string peep.

8. If you have access to suitable scales, measure the major and minor draw weights. Your owner's manual should be checked before changing draw weight. Adjust the two-wheeled compound; turn in

Using the Golden Key Targetmaster Shoot-thru Arrowrest

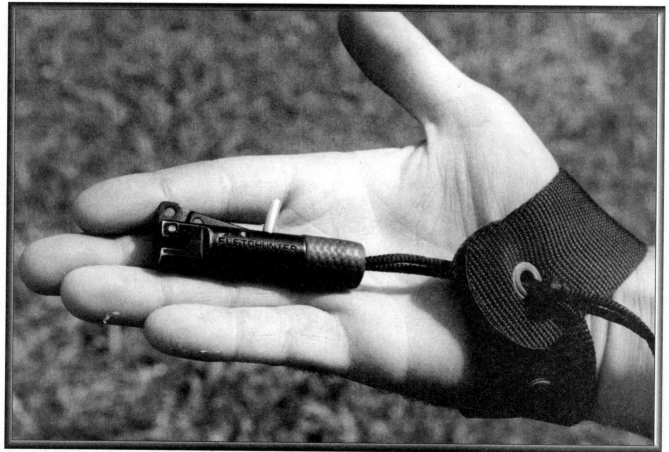

A hardnose release compliments "straight line nocking". I feel that a wrist supported release permits the best control of a mechanical release. Shown is the Wrist Drawn Fletchunter by Jim Fletcher Archery Aids Inc.

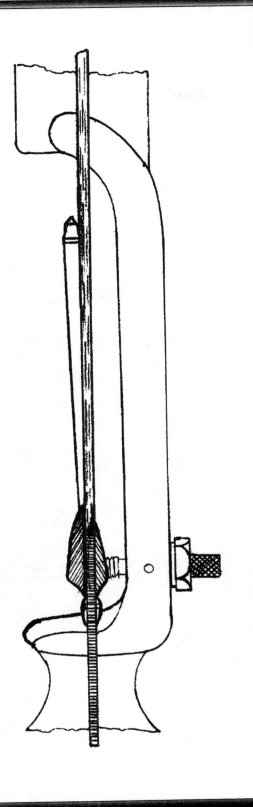

DETERMINING ARROW OFFSET

STEP No. 1

Select a location permitting you to lean your bow and nocked arrow in a near vertical position.

STEP No. 2

Stand several feet behind the bow. Align the bowstring with the center of both bowlimbs and sight down the arrow.

STEP No. 3

The tip of the arrow and the bowstring shown in the drawing is a reasonable offset for your starting point.

STEP No. 4

Some experienced release shooters approach "Dead Center." The arrowtip and the center of the bowstring are almost in alignment. Finger shooters generally require more nock height and offset.

STEP No. 5

Broadheads require more offset and nock height than field points.

the adjustments to increase draw weight or back them out to decrease it. Move the screws in tandem, alternating one turn per screw. Upon reaching the desired draw weight, recheck the tiller height. If it is unequal, try jiggling the weight adjustment screws. It is best to turn the screws equally. If you have to turn one screw to achieve equal tiller height, make it a one-quarter or one-half turn. Placing the socket head screws in equal alignment makes weight adjustment easy by increasing or reducing limb pressure.

9. Install a cable guard. It's best to use a suitable bow press. If you don't have one, relax the limbs by backing out the weight adjustment screws. About eight turns should relax the limbs enough to make the installation. Don't back out the screws

Shooting off the shelf

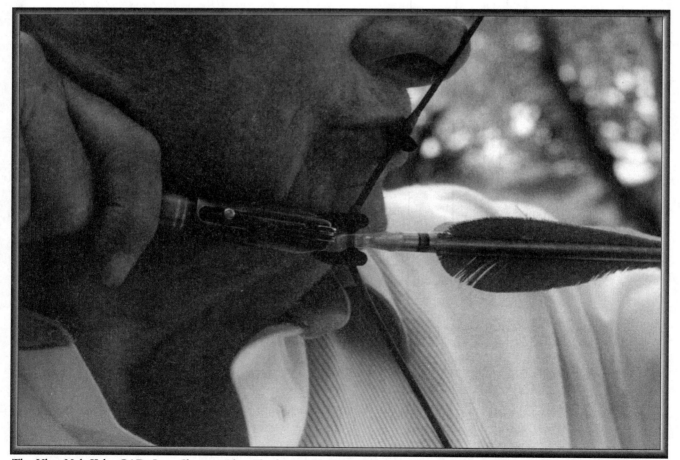

The Ultra-Nok II by QAD, Inc. Shown with a Fletchunter Hardnose Release. This device provides a quicker paradox recovery and better arrow flight. It is a real advantage with the newer extremely short bows.

completely. Check the owner's manual to see on which side of the cable guard the cables should be located.

Tighten the draw weight screws one turn at a time until reaching the desired weight and tiller. With a nocked arrow in place, lean the bow against a table and sight down the arrow. If you are a release shooter, look at the inside hen feather and the nearest cable the feather will pass when shot. Try for 1/8-inch clearance by rotating the cable guard. If you shoot fingers, try 3/16-inch clearance. If the hen feather starts to look fuzzy, it is touching the cable and the clearance should be increased.

10. *It takes 100 to 125 shots to shoot-in a bow. Set the in-out position of the arrow rest. Assuming a*

Using a gauge to determine arrow offset.

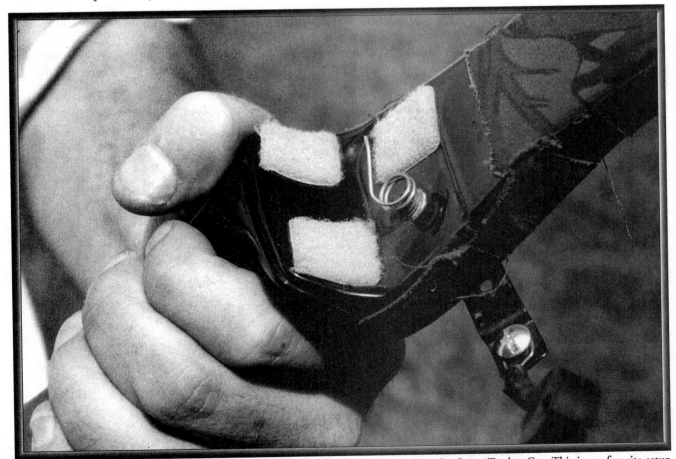

Using Velcro to prevent unwanted sound. A springy arrowrest and a "spare finger" by the Game Tracker Co. This is my favorite setup when hunting from a tree and using aluminum arrows fletched with feathers.

reasonable spine and a mechanical release, you can approach string alignment center easier with a light point rather than a heavy one.

If you are going 3-D shooting, you can also lower the nock height and gain some velocity until you begin having erratic arrow flight. Remember that 3-D is reasonably flat and level. If you plan to shoot broadheads, you will need a little paradox and a little height to the nocking point. If you are 20 feet up in a tree and one of the sons of "Old Many Points" sneaks in behind and makes it almost under your nose before you can risk a draw, the only thought in your mind should be that you hope the safety belt holds. A little nock high is good security for that odd-angle shot. Arrow rest clearance is a necessity for accuracy in such shots — an arrow hitting an arrow rest can mean a devastating miss.

11. Set the arrow rest spring tension. For draw weights up to 40 pounds, select light to firm for light target arrows, and use a firm setting for field or hunting weight arrows. If the bow draws 40 to 60 pounds, choose a firmer setting; use a stiff setting for 60 pounds and over.

Some archers like the cushion plunger style of rest. The cushion plunger has yet to show me anything but a moveable device that can vary in its ability to move. You may like it, though. Most shoot-thru rests offer the option of using two pieces of slip-over tubing. The tubing can affect the way the arrow sits in the rest, and, because of wear, change the point of impact. The change is very gradual.

Fine tuning arrow flight once meant having a friend stand behind you to observe its trajectory. Times and arrow velocity have changed to the

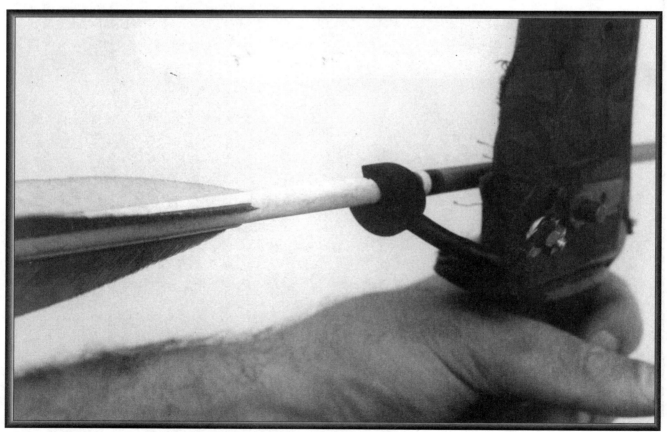

The "spare finger" holding an arrow in place while waiting for game.

Using a measured arrow to determine draw length

Using a "Bow Stringer" is the safe way for the archer and the bow

point where it's impossible to pinpoint the problem with an arrow traveling 280 to 300 plus feet per second. Paper tuning seems to be very popular since cuts in a paper leave no doubt as to what's going on. The last five bows that were unpacked in my shop included instructions for paper tuning, which is good as long as the archer doesn't become obsessed with seeking absolute perfection.

Paper tuning refers to tears left in paper by an arrow. If the paper tear indicates nock high, lower the nocking point. If the tear is nock left, try the next stiffer arrow. If the tear is nock right, try an arrow with a weaker spine. Each tear, of course, can have more than one cause. While the tear pattern indicates just what is happening, the true payoff is a good group at a target 20 or more yards away. Don't get so wrapped up in paper tuning that you lose confidence because the tear pattern is not perfect.

Now is a good time to tighten the temporary settings and apply a few turns of dental floss. Make sure your arrows are in good shape. Number them so you can determine quickly if something unusual has happened to only one of them. Watch for wear marks on the edge of a feather. Be leery of dark marks that show up on the edge of a vane. Deliberately take the bow out of tiller one limb at a time to see what happens. Don't be afraid to experiment, but work out a system so that you can always return to the original settings.

You are in command of the bow, and you can make it do your bidding. From now on, that good feeling you get when you face a target or spot "Old Many Points" slipping along is confidence-building within yourself. Isn't it a great feeling? ▲

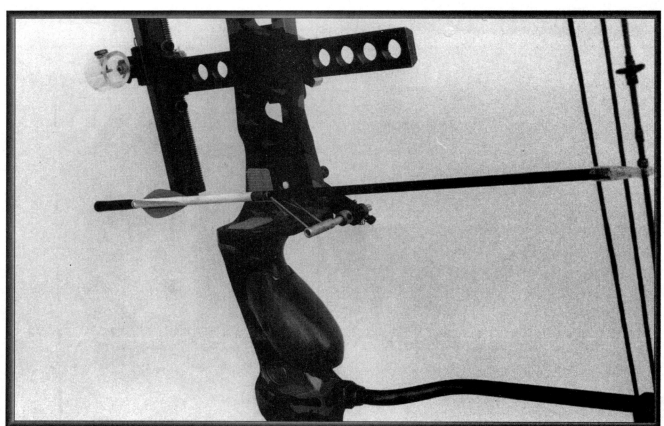

Using a short piece of broken arrow to check vane and arrowrest clearance.

CHAPTER TEN

Accuracy Aids On The Bow String

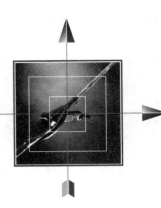

Talking about a bow string in a book about the modern bow may seem unusual, so an explanation is in order. A good bow string ties it all together. A well positioned nocking point that remains in position, a kisser button that stays put, and a string peep that maintains an accurate relationship with the bow sight must all work together to create a piece of equipment that can produce accuracy. Until the arrival of the flat-limbed recurve bow and the Dacron-brand of polyester filament bow string, keeping accurate shooting aids in a dependable relationship was a full-time project.

England and Western Europe established target archery as we know it. Flax made the best

Martin Speed demons mounted on a bowstring to dampen string oscillations. The high energy cams show the most improvement.

A Fine-Line Zero Peer anchored to a bow cable. Courtesy Hawk Assoc. and Fine-Line.

bow strings until the arrival of Dacron. Did you know that flax was often woven into linen? The reputation of Irish linen as a high-quality fabric is well known, so the British Isles could well have been the home of the flax bow string until its replacement by hemp

As a first cousin of hemp, flax has probably produced its share of bow strings. Hemp was first used to make high quality rope; it was, in fact, the rope of choice of Judge Parker's hangman at Fort Smith, Arkansas, just before the turn of the century. Because it was the best material available, hemp served archers well for many years. Because hemp stretches, maintaining a constant fistmele

meant checking at the end of each round of arrows. The nock point relationship to the arrow rest changed constantly. Kisser button and string peep height stretched so far that many archers felt they were more trouble than they were worth. Among my archery paraphernalia is a factory-made hemp bow string with a formed sliding loop.

The arrival of the fiberglass wood-laminated bow and the Dacron string made the double-looped, continuous-strand bow string possible. The Dacron filament was the first bow string with very low stretch and permitted the use of dependable fixed accuracy aids.

The first permanent nock point installed was formed from a well-known brand of waxed dental floss. The next innovation was the brass- or plastic-lined ring that clamped around the bow string. The Saunders Archery Company product works best with a monofilament center serving. Clamping on with a medium pressure will allow you to run the ring up or down by twisting the ring around the center serving until the desired height is reached. The monofilament serving acts much like threads on machine screws to raise or lower the nock height.

I measure nocking point heights with a "bow square." The arrow rest and arrow diameter often dictate the type of square that I choose. If the front of the arrow is equipped with a screw-in insert or outsert, I'll use a square by BPE Inc. This square is at its best with the use of a shoot-thru arrow rest and a small diameter arrow shaft. If glue-in points are used, you may have to promote a 12- to 14-inch piece of shaft of the same size and install an insert or outsert.

The metal Potawatome bow square is handy if the arrow rest is a shelf or a flipper rest is used. This bow square can be relieved to provide clearance over a kisser button, which lies only a short distance from the nocking point. My sons razz me

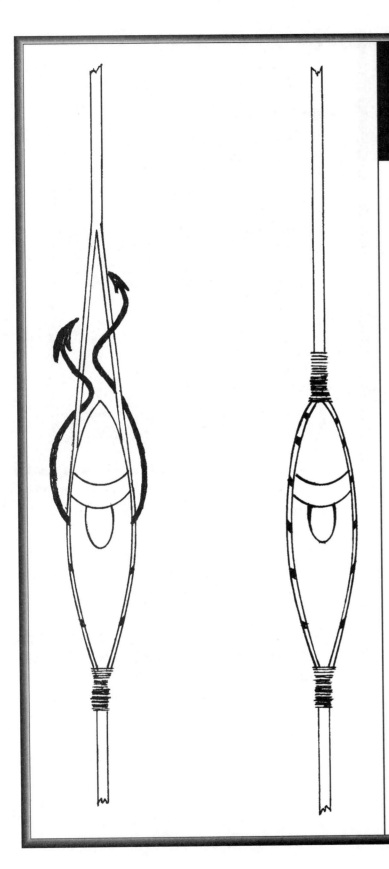

SECURING A STRINGPEEP IN YOUR BOWSTRING

A. *Divide bowstring into two equal groups of strands. A blunt screwdriver can do an excellent job. Do not damage bowstring.*

B. *Slip stringpeep into the spread bowstring strands. Draw bow and determine height of stringpeep hole. Measure and record this height above nocking point.*

C. *Be very generous with dental floss and pull the bowstring together at the bottom of the stringpeep. Secure this binding leaving two lengths of floss long enough to spiral around the bowstring strands and pull the strands together at the top of the stringpeep.*

The Concealed End Binding works very well to secure your peep. You have used a spiral wrap to join the dental floss lashings together and doubled your holding power. Today's bowstring Super Fibers have also proven to be super slick

A Factory produced hemp bowstring.

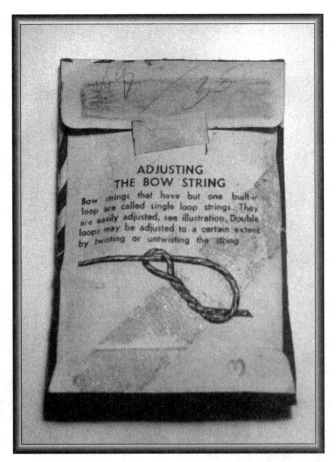

The knot used to adjust fistmele when using a hemp bowstring.

about using one with a string peep, but sometimes "Old Many Points" slips in behind me at the base of my tree. When this happens, the kisser button slides between my lips and emboldens me to make this father-to-sons comment:

"Boys, that is what you are here for. Now drag him out to the truck."

A kisser button is small plastic disk that is available in two sizes to fit large and small bow strings. It is held in place by two small metal clamps that can be tightened only by sliding the button up and down the bow string until it has a natural feel as it slides between your lips. Kisser buttons are available at archery shops and from the Game/Tracker Company.

A string peep is a plastic device that comes in a variety of shapes and sizes. It does for a bow string what a receiver sight does for a rifle. The peep hole can range from 1/16 of an inch to 1/4 inch; some are elongated for ultra short bows. String peeps work because the human eye naturally concentrates on the light that comes through their openings, a phenomenon that produces an extremely accurate alignment of the light center, the sight pin and the target. String peep openings can be round, oval, elliptical, square or diamond shaped. The openings can be as large as 1/4 inch; anything above that will hurt accuracy.

I favor the Zero Peep from Fineline for all types of shooting. The standard peep hole is drilled to a 9/64 diameter for bowhunting. The opening is as large as possible without threatening the sight's structural strength. Recently, Fineline expanded its line by adding a number of sizes up to 1/4 inch. The peeps depend on a rubber tube to rotate the bow string and orient the peep and the bow string. The tube should be replaced at the start of the bow season and again when spring tournament shooting begins.

Cut a narrow strip of masking tape using the srting-peep hole as a gauge. Start several inches above your nocking point and spiral-wrap the masking tape. Set a sightpin at 30-35 yards and draw to your normal anchor point. Your master eye will appear to be looking thru the spiral wrapped portion of the bowstring and aligning the sight pin and the target. The spiral wrapping makes it easy to approximate a point on your bowstring. Measure from the bottom of your nocking point to this mark. This distance is the height of the string-peep center above the bottom of your nocking point.

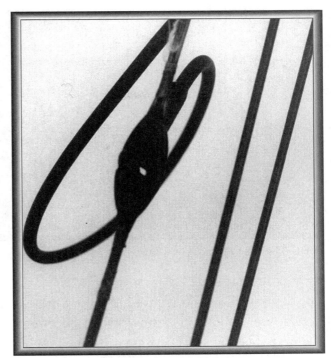

A "Stringpeep" provides additional accuracy.

A Mississippi River Island produced this bow harvested gobbler.

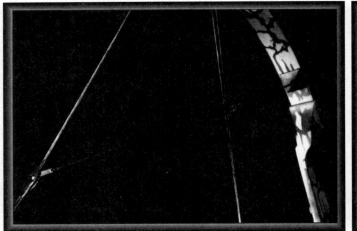
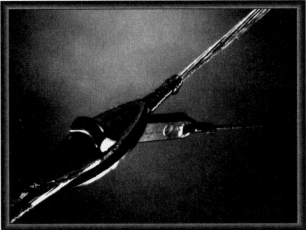

A Fine-Line Zero 11 Peepsight mounted in a bowstring. Courtesy Hawk Adv. and Fine-Line.

Measure the distance from the bottom of the nocking point to the center of the peep. Relax the bow string, remove the string divider and insert the peep, making sure there are the same number of strands in the groves on each side of the peep. The plastic tube projection attaches one end of the rubber tube to a cable on the bow. Use a minimum of stretch to align the peep. Fineline's new 1/4-inch diameter peep may at first seem to be too large, but with a little practice you'll find that it works well. Because the short bows produced this year create a very sharp bow string angle, you may want to elongate the peep hole. In order to protect an expensive bow string from damage, it's a good idea to remove the peep from the bow string before tackling this job. Use a small rattail finishing file to enlarge the opening.

I find that using a string peep settles me down and coordinates the anchor point and sight pin. It seems to help me squeeze off a better-placed shot. Many bowhunters put themselves at a disadvantage by using a peep hole that is too small. Small holes may improve accuracy if you're standing on two well-braced legs shooting at a well-lit target on a level shooting range, but not when the scene changes to a dense alder thicket in the Colorado Rockies with the light growing dim as the sun slides behind a mountain peak and the target is a very bugled trophy elk, tearing up 3-inch alders 25 yards down range.

That mental picture may have popped into your mind frequently over the years. You even have a spot picked out for the antlers. At that moment, all the elk has on its mind is locating the challenger on his turf and sending him on his way. When that happens, you are indeed living one of the top hunting experiences North America has to offer. To make that vision of a trophy come true, you need all the light you can get. A tiny little hole that dims the shooting light could ruin that dream. ▲

A "Kisser Button" provides added security for that difficult bowhunting shot.

CHAPTER ELEVEN

Using The Bow Sight

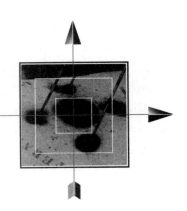

The first bow sights were basic, probably a simple elevation control created to help European archers defend their castles, firing from on high at invading ground forces. With many of their shots as long as 100 yards, a mark on the bow helped archers get on target quickly. I'm willing to bet that the distances on the castle grounds were marked off to help defenders hit their target.

During the Middle Ages, many European lords required their vassals to meet each Sunday afternoon for archery practice, something like today's weekend training sessions for reservists and the National Guard. The gatherings were serious business, not fun-and-games shooting; archers had to hit the mark or explain why they didn't. Europe was home to the accurate long bow, and archery was the first line of defense; it's logical to conclude the bow sight originated here. Firearms eventually replaced bows, but they never brought the pleasure that comes from launching arrows. The days of forced Sunday

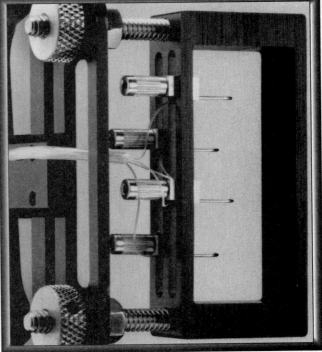

Two views of the Fine-line Fiber Optic 'Ultra-Glo': left photo, right handed archer; right photo, left handed archer. Courtesy Hawk Assoc. and Fine-Line.

practice sessions eventually evolved into a few devoted archers taking pleasure in their sport.

Between World Wars I and II, several small groups of devoted target archers scattered across the United State created what is known today as the National Archery Association. This organization developed the regulations that brought U.S. archers into international competition and formed a nucleus of instructors to serve the Boy Scouts and college-level archery competitors.

Hunting films produced by Pope and Young before World War II fed the growth of archery as a sport. Howard Hill contributed to this growth with his popular short-subject archery films that promoted sport archery. And then Ben Pearson, an active target archer who produced equipment sold through sporting

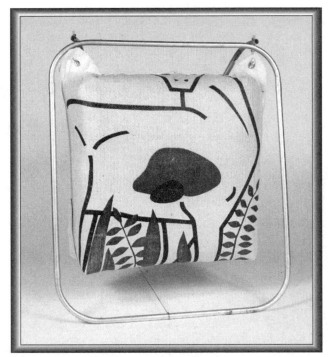

Targets that help develop your shooting skills.

A Morrell Eternity Target handles your field and target arrows.

goods stores. By the start of World War II, a number of young archers, all quite serious about target shooting and bowhunting, organized the National Field Archery Association, whereupon the sport took off like a rocket.

In the late 1940s and early '50s, archery competition became popular in Europe, especially England, but the sport drew little interest in areas still recovering from the war. International and Olympic archery drew few teams until the 1980s and '90s. Whereas target shooting requires a bow sight, the growing number of young archers in the United States preferred field archery competition, which they considered practice for their real love, bow-hunting. They knew little about the bow sight and happily acknowledged that a sight was the best way to miss a deer. It was, in their eyes, a gadget for sissies and old target archers.

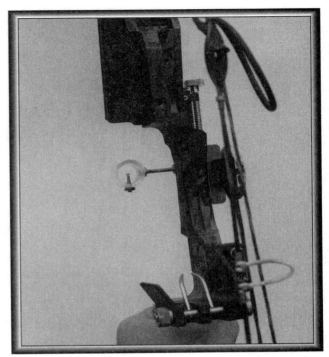

A view of a single pin bowsight.

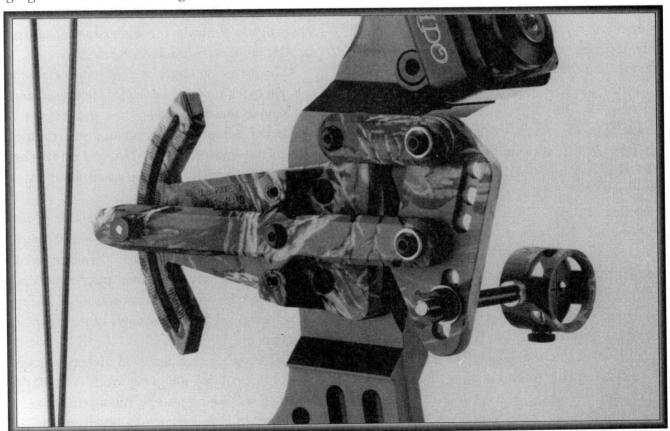

The Sight Master, a single pin sight with quick easy adjustments. Courtesy Hawk Assoc. and Sight Master Inc.

These 3-D targets help develop your range estimating skills.

The growth of the National Archery Association and its influence in the promotion and regulation of Olympic and international competition gave the United States a dominate role in those contests. International competition, meanwhile allowed only a simple pin sight that was adjustable for windage and elevation. That was as complicated as it could get. Early bow sights were usually mounted on the face or back of the wooden handle riser. Bow sights mounted on the side of the handle riser often produced a built-in windage error that had to be corrected by shimming the mounting block. The misalignment of the handle riser was common on early handmade bows, a problem that could recur today as handmade bows again become popular. Check for this misalignment on any compound or recurve bow with a side-mounted sight. For example, when a sight pin is moved up or down on a bow in vertical alignment at 30 yards, you'll notice a windage change on one side or the other of the sight pin.

Today's metal handle riser has largely eliminated this error, but the following checks can help increase your score or boost your chances of bagging a critter:

1. *Number or mark all arrows and check them for windage alignment problems. If you find that one of them repeatedly strikes out of windage alignment, check it for straightness, nock alignment and damage. If it continues to strike out of the group but appears safe to use for small game, go ahead.*

2.. *Make sure the arrows are properly spined. If several arrows with similar spine markings are on target at close range but miss at greater distance - and the only adjustment is elevation of the sight — a spine problem seems likely.*

3. *If your sight has screws that permit horizontal adjustment of the vertical sight bar, the solution can be as simple as moving the top of the vertical sight bar a small distance. Pulling the sign pin into the sight window will move the arrow impact away from the sight window. Pushing the top of the vertical sight bar away from the sight windows moves the arrow impact toward the sight window. Lock the holding screws tightly. Return to the shorter range and reset the sight pin for both windage and elevation.*

4. *If you are on target at close range, move the sight pin to the elevation setting for the longer range and resume shooting, making sure that the arrow impact and sight pin windage adjustment are oriented to the same vertical plane. The sight pin windage adjustment should be the same at all distances — unless you're shooting in a cross wind.*

5. *If no adjustment screws are available, loosen the mounting block and correct the misalignment with shim stock spacers. Allen flat-head screws provide the best mounting block attachment. Coat the holding screws with a small amount of silicone fishing reel grease to ease removal of the mounting block later on.*

While bowhunting and field archery enjoyed spurts in popularity following World War II, the bow sight still got no respect. Attempting to use a bow sight on a slower recurve bow typically led someone to ask where the archer expected to find

Targets #1-2-#3-#4 are for target or field points only.

a deer that would stand around waiting until the hunter estimated the range and set his sight. With the arrival of the compound bow and its faster arrows, the bow sight and slip release finally made it into the game woods. Several states outlawed the use of the release until its growing popularity forced acceptance (Arkansas still bars the use of any magnification in a bow sight).

Once the National Field Archery Association legalized the mechanical release for competition, field archers grabbed them as fast as factories could turn them out, and the bow sight became more than a "simple pin." As the compound became the bow of choice among North America's beginning archers, the demand grew for a bow sight that improved accuracy at longer ranges. Bowhunters preferred a simple bracket that held about five fixed pins. They could be set for ranges from 10 to 50 yards at 10-yard increments. Bowhunters like to talk about their success and misses, begging the question: "Would you believe that I chose the wrong pin?" They continued to experiment with bow cast, moving some multi-pin setups closer together until they formed a tight cluster. On rare occasions, a bowhunter would admit aiming and missing with the entire pin cluster.

Tightening of the multi-pin sight blotted out so much of the game animal that bowhunters started looking for other sighting devices. Among the first improvements was to eliminate one of the sight pins. Armed with a carbon shaft, lightweight broadheads and better bow cast, many bowhunters dropped the fourth pin for better visibility and used instead a three-point set in 20-, 40- and 50-yard segments.

Sight pins are now available tipped with several different materials and come in several sizes. Colored Fiberoptic and translucent plastic tips are quite popular. Many top-scoring 3-D shooters use small diameter metal pins, which pay off with greater target visibility and an ability to hold tighter on the smaller X-ring.

One group of successful bowhunters I know about uses three or four different sight pin tips painted in highly visible but nonreflective colors. The sight is mounted on a fast bow that shoots helical feather-fletched carbon arrows tipped with a glue-on three-blade Muzzy or Razorback broadhead. One look at this bow and you'll know instinctively that it can cast an arrow fast and flat. A closer inspection will likely show that the owner uses his sight pins as range finders or as a check on his estimate of the distance. When a bowhunter starts his draw, he can judge the distance to the target by how much of the animal's body is blocked out by the pins.

It takes a lot of range shooting to learn how to work with the sight pins, but they'll reward you with increased accuracy. Think of the sight pin as an instrument for triangulation. From the top of a doe's back to the bottom of her stomach measures about 12 inches. As the distance increases, the doe will appear to shrink, requiring smaller pin openings. A large diameter pin is

Dale Morrell displays his Eternity Target.

fine at 30 yards, but you'll need a medium at 40 yards and a small at 50 yards. Although a buck with antlers may be somewhat larger, the difference will have little effect on arrow impact until you reach distances of 50 or 60 yards. Elk, with their large chests, require adjustments. Baited bear are generally considered short-range game; you usually know the distance before climbing into the stand.

The fixed multi-pin sight is both inexpensive and dependable, making it today's most popular. It also helps that the pins are adjustable for windage at a set distance, which helps keep the arrows in the same vertical plane. For most beginning bowhunters, this is the sight of choice.

The next step up is a bracket sight with a side-mounted sight bar. The sight bar ties into a crossover bar supporting a sturdy bracket with as many as five wires for adjusting elevation, plus a vertical wire for windage adjustment. The crossover bar also provides an additional windage adjustment for the bracket. The sighting intersections inside the bracket can be made of metal or translucent plastic. The improved visibility offered by the bracket site seems to be a real asset in holding on the 3-D X-ring or on game. Translucent plastic gives an

unusual but welcome amount of sight visibility at dawn and dusk without the brilliance of a colored sight intersection that can overwhelm the view of game.

It's a good idea to carry two brackets, one with a wire intersection for the 3-D range and one with a plastic intersection for hunting. During the hunting season, sight-in both brackets for broadheads and you'll have a spare in case of a disaster. You might also keep the wire bracket sighted-in for field points and indoor night league tournaments. Be careful with them, though. Bracket sights may look sturdy, but a brush with a limb or brush can knock them out of adjustment.

Before buying a crossover bar, make sure it's long enough to accommodate the larger sight window clearance on newer bows. Some sight makers have fallen behind bowyers who've increased the sight window cutout to allow for overdraw arrow rests. I'm confident that bow sight producers will soon catch up.

The world's most advanced bow sight is an old favorite of U.S. target archers. The single-pin adjustable tournament sight has brought home the gold for this nation many times. Bill Hogue got me started with the Check-It single pin target sight, and Keith Stuart tipped me off to

A 3-D target of a deer.

LEARNING TO USE A SINGLE SIGHT PIN

STEP NO. 1

Sight in at 30-35 yards. Use broadheads and a target recommended for broadheads.
Without changing your sight pin setting move up to 20 yards.

STEP NO. 2

You are looking for a sight pin setting that should not exceed a 12 inch trajectory height at
20 yards or anywhere along the remaining distance to your sight pin setting.

STEP NO. 3

The 50-60 pound bow shooting 125 grain broadheads with medium to heavy arrows will have difficulty
attaining a 12 inch 20 yard trajectory with a 30-35 yard sight pin setting. Heavier bows, light broadheads,
carbonshafts, and reducing your forward of center percentage can exceed that 30-35 yard sight pin range. What
ever equipment you choose stay with the maximum 12 inch trajectory when measured at 20 yards regardless of
your sight pin setting. With a little experience you can adapt this 12 inch trajectory to hunting almost any animal.

STEP NO. 4

Having arrived at a certain sight pin setting familiarize yourself with this setting. At close range you will hold
low. At your pin setting range you will hold "dead on" or to minimize range estimation error holding just under
the animal's back will still produce a hit. If the animal is closer than estimated you still have a good chance and
if it is further the arrow can hit low in the chest cavity. If you realize that the animal is further than your fixed
sight pin range learn to think of holdover in terms of the animal's chest width.

STEP NO. 5

Merely setting your equipment to hit 12 inches high at 20 yards and skipping the 30-35 yard shooting can fail
to reveal some wind planing problems with your arrow. The longer shooting will help develop you shooting skill.

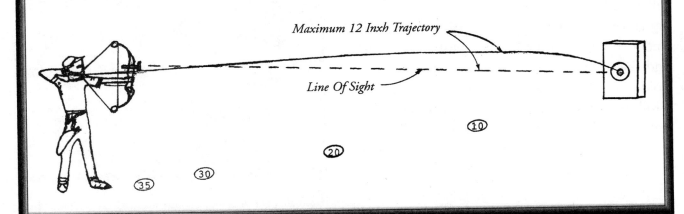

Maximum 12 Inxh Trajectory

Line Of Sight

the Hot Shot mechanical release for hunting. I've used these sights on my bow ever since Any time I think that it will improve my shooting, I change a sight pin. Archers who have not tried the single pin system seemingly search for reasons to avoid it. They like to place their sight pin directly on the desired point of arrow impact, prompting the "Old Bowhunter's" comment about choosing the wrong sight pin.

Too many bowhunters concentrate on archery practice but they seldom practice range estimation. The trick is to estimate 40 yards accurately. Once single-pin shooters learn to make their equipment work for them, they become converts. Go to a shooting area and sight-in for 40 yards. Without changing the sight setting, shoot another group at 20 yards. Measure the arrow impact above the aiming point, looking for a 12-inch height. If you're hitting higher than 12 inches, cut back to a 35-yard setting and try again (remember, 12 inches is the usual distance from the top of a doe to the bottom of her stomach; use that as a walking gauge for selecting the aiming and impact point).

Plot a trajectory chart and study your arrow impacts at 10, 20, 30 and 40 yards. If your arrow is rising at 10 yards with a 40-yard sight pin setting, lower the desired arrow impact by half a deer's body. At 20 yards, you'll still have a killing shot with a flat-shooting bow. At 30 yards, your arrow will drop slightly, so hold just under the stomach line. Forty yards is dead-on and the arrow will begin to drop. At 45 yards, hold to the top of the animal's back; at 50 yards, a full deer's chest above the back can still bag the critter. If you are in heavy cover where 20 yards may be the longest shot, set the adjustable pin for 20 yards; at 30 yards, set for that distance. In more open areas, use a 35- to 40-yard setting.

Beyond a setting of 40 yards, the margin of error disappears rapidly for both closer and longer ranges. A 50-yard kill requires a skilled archer with an efficient flying arrow and a fast bow. The arrow must be a thin-wall aluminum or carbon shaft with a minimum helical fletch that has been tested with broadheads for dependable flight. They should be balanced out to about 13 percent forward of center to produce a flat flight.

If you think from reading this chapter that I prefer the single pin adjustable sight over all others, you're right. I have several Chek-It sights on the bows that I use. My youngest son Rayburn grew up using this sight and asks me for "a lime-green pin extending down from the top of the sight ring." My second son Travis is a bow sight experimenter who shoots a PSE Mongoose equipped with translucent plastic. When the spring 3-D season begins, he changes to small diameter metallic wires. He even ordered a fire-pink pin that rises from the bottom of the sight ring. It wasn't long before he asks, *"Pop, could you install a level?"*

Here we go again!

A Fine-Line Crosshair Bow Sight. This sight was a pioneer for the crosshair sight. It is very popular today. Courtesy Hawk Assoc. and Fine-Line.

CHAPTER TWELVE

A Little Arrow History

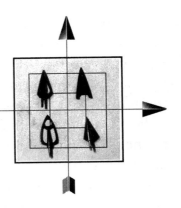

It's easy to imagine ancient hunters setting fire to long, thin sticks and sending them high into the air as they whiled away their time around the campfire. They competed to see who could send the flaming drills higher or farther, modifying the sticks and launching equipment to get an advantage in the contests. Their efforts led to the first crude bows, and arrows, adequate enough for them, perhaps, but far removed from today's equipment.

Until the 1930s, arrows were made of wood; Port Orford cedar competed for a while, but aluminum arrows and shafts soon became king. I have in my collection an

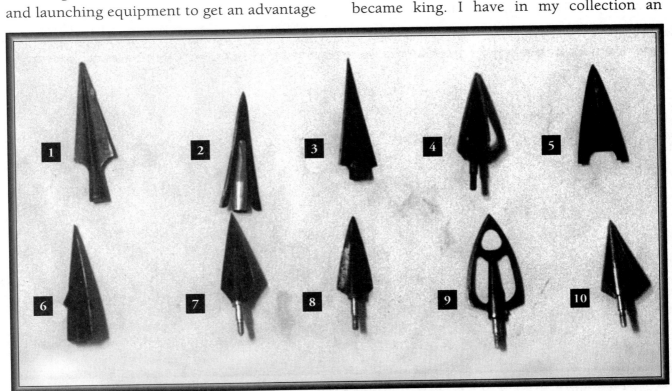

Since the nineteen-thirties broadhead arrow points have had many design and material changes. 1- A cast steel point by Ben Pearson. 2- A prewar point by Howard Hill. 3- A steel blade mounted in plastic by Hilbre. 4- The familiar Bear Razorhead is available in both tool and stainless steel. 5- A head constructed of tool steel. This head has a very light and strong pressed ferrule by Ben Pearson. 6- A tool steel blade mounted in plastic by Rose City Archery. 7- A very advanced tool steel design by John Zwickey. 8- A very early designed three blade head MA-3. 9- The "Deadhead" by Ben Pearson. 10- A replaceable three blade head by Savora.

arrow from the last dozen wood competition target arrows owned by the late Ben Pearson. That was shortly before he changed to the popular blue multi-ring design that he used until his death. It has a barreled, tapered cedar shaft footed with Arkansas hickory and a nock made of laminated tropical hardwoods. My arrow has a hole from the nock to the footing, either an attempt by Pearson to cut its weight or the result of a spine-control experiment.

When Doug Easton fletched his first aluminum arrow, he was one among many such producers, but his early products were too soft and bent on impact. He eventually learned to stiffen them by a process that remains a secret of the Easton Company. The introduction of the aluminum arrow ran into immediate opposition from those who saw it as a violation of tradition. In competitions, though, those who fired aluminum arrows consistently outscored archers who stuck with wood. As a result, aluminum quickly became the standard.

When World War II ended, the giant aluminum factories that had produced military equipment tried making arrows as a way to keep busy. They knew aluminum but they didn't know archery, and those who purchased their products spent as much time straightening the arrows as they did shooting them. Meanwhile, the Easton Company built on its technological advantage and expanded into such products as tent poles and canoe paddles. The company, however, remains committed to making the world's best arrows. ▲

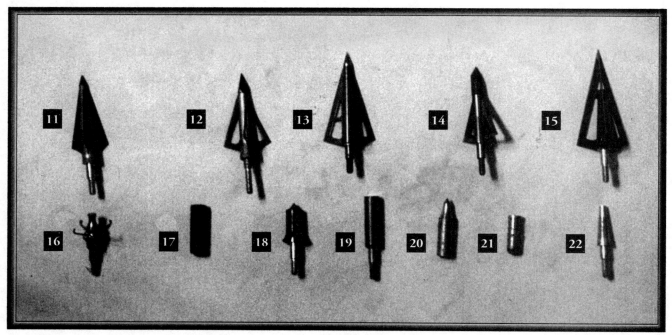

11- A replaceable three blade head by Satellite. 12- A replaceable three blade head with angled blades and a cutting tip by Kolpin. 13- A large replaceable blade the "Rocky Mountain Supreme" by Bob Barrie. 14- A replaceable four blade head with a cutting tip by Muzzy. 15- A super strong three fixed blade head by Roger Rothhaar called the "Snuffer." 16- A famous small game and roving head named the "Zwickey Judo." 17- Another small game blunt and roving head. 18- A screw-in blunt head for small game named the "Game Nabber." 19- A screw-in blunt for small game. 20- A taperhole target and field point. 21- An adapter to mount points using the screw-in feature. 22- A screw-in mounting for heads using a taperhole ferrule.

CHAPTER THIRTEEN

Arrow Points And Small Game

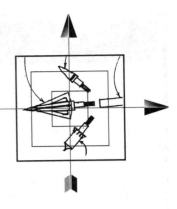

The first "bow" consisted of a piece of rawhide, sinew, vine or the like stretched tightly between the ends of a limb. It was used first to spin sticks against dry wood so rapidly that friction brought the kindling to the ignition point, providing ancient man with fire. Archaeologists have discovered evidence of the practice world-wide, an indication that the bow was "invented" many times in many places. One of the more curious among these prehistoric people laid a fire drill across the bow, drew it back and let go, gazing in awe as the arrow flew into the air. Thus was archery born!

Logic indicates that the first archer tried various ways to control the "fire drill." Tired of

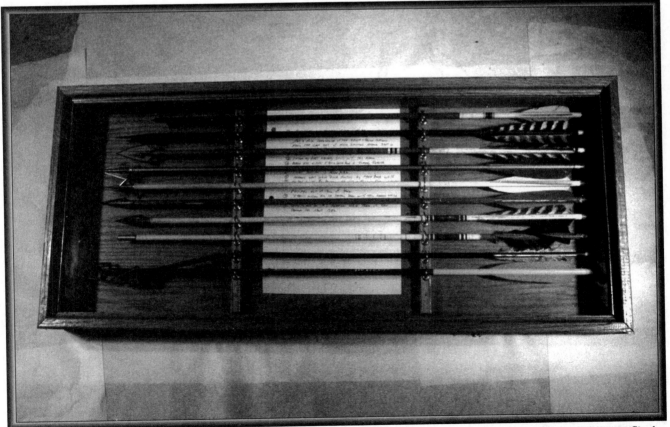

An archer should have a method of saving and displaying arrows that have a story to tell. These arrows become more treasured as time flies by.

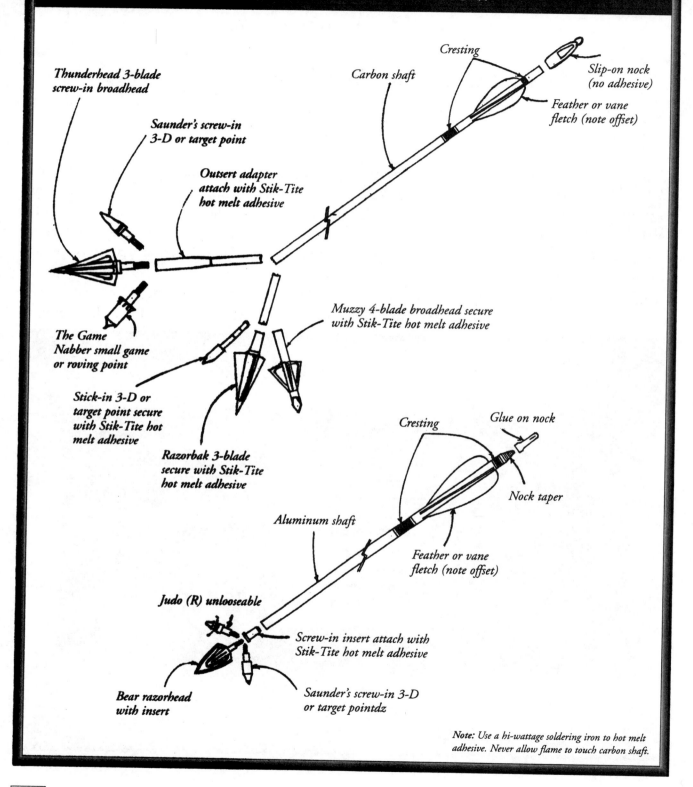

Thunderhead 3-blade screw-in broadhead

Saunder's screw-in 3-D or target point

Outsert adapter attach with Stik-Tite hot melt adhesive

Cresting

Carbon shaft

Slip-on nock (no adhesive)

Feather or vane fletch (note offset)

The Game Nabber small game or roving point

Muzzy 4-blade broadhead secure with Stik-Tite hot melt adhesive

Stick-in 3-D or target point secure with Stik-Tite hot melt adhesive

Razorbak 3-blade secure with Stik-Tite hot melt adhesive

Cresting

Glue on nock

Nock taper

Aluminum shaft

Feather or vane fletch (note offset)

Judo (R) unlooseable

Screw-in insert attach with Stik-Tite hot melt adhesive

Bear razorhead with insert

Saunder's screw-in 3-D or target pointdz

Note: Use a hi-wattage soldering iron to hot melt adhesive. Never allow flame to touch carbon shaft.

seeing how far or high he could send his arrows, he aimed them at moving targets. The first scurrying critter felled by one of those blunt projectiles was a victim of the first bowhunter, who soon learned to use his crude bows and arrows to protect himself and his family from intruders. When he learned that penetrating tips attached to the front of the arrows greatly improved their effectiveness, he began a search for better points. Today's successors to those crude flying fire drills provide modern man with sport, food and defense.

Bows and arrows merely provided early man with an interesting diversion. Then he developed tips for his arrows, turning them into weapons for hunting or long-distance defense. Over the centuries, arrow points were made from a variety of materials and formed into a number of interesting shapes.

Sporting Arrow Points

Bowhunters have always met their problems head on. Over the many years since early man developed bows and arrows, the types of arrow points have emerged to fit hunters' needs.

Pre-World War II bowhunters and archers typically had a set of broadheads and target arrows to use for shooting. But bowhunters at the time found that neither broadheads nor target points were practical for the type of roaming archery that was gaining in popularity.

It was soon learned, however, that empty brass cases from .38 Special cartridges made blunt point serviceable for the common 11/32" wood arrowshaft.

Once the five-degree tapered ferrule for broadheads made its appearance, the factory-built taper hole blunt point was soon to follow. This created a demand for the tapered hole target point, and within a short time these two types of points were available in a choice of weights, making it easy to change an arrow to any use desired. Changing point types was accomplished with the use of a hot-melt cement commonly used to repair bamboo fishing rods. This laid the groundwork for the screw-in replaceable point in future years.

Early aluminum arrow shaft material was still too soft for anything but target shooting into straw or baled excelsior. The arrival of the XX75

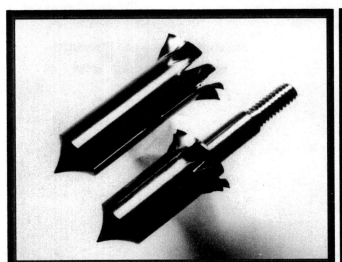 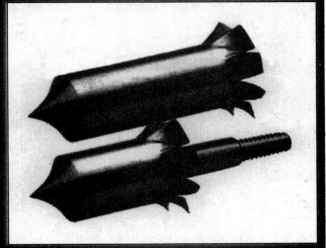

The Game Nabber points fits woodshafts or screw-in aluminum and carbonshafts. It is an excellent small game point. Courtesy Keith Jabben of Precision Designed Products.

alloy made the screw-in insert a practical piece of equipment and became standard equipment almost overnight. Glue-in target points became available for aluminum and carbon shafts. They are best installed with the new Bohning STIK-TITE hot melt (made especially for carbon shafts). Use a high wattage soldering iron to heat the metal points when installing the points on carbon shafts; but do so without applying heat to the carbon shaft. STIK-TITE can also be used to install inserts or outserts for screw-in points on aluminum or carbon arrow shafts (epoxy should be considered for permanent installation).

A newer type of point that has almost made the blunt obsolete is the Zwickey Judo®. The Judo point features four spring steel fingers

Two old Gar Shooting Gig Heads made by Bill Clements and myself. The old Stingray Single Point Head is still very modern by any standard.

This Alligator GAR shot by Fred Thorn while Kelly Morse handled the boat should not be called small game. Note Thorn's use of the "Retriever Reel". Courtesy Fred Thorn.

projecting outward from a coil spring, which can cause the arrow to flip up and remain visible to the archer. Called the "unloseable arrow," the Judo is quite effective on small game, and the wire fingers seem to protect the shaft from bending or breaking. The steel fingers prevent complete penetration and increase hemorrhaging with the arrow impact.

A similar point — the Muzzy Grasshopper — has projecting wire fingers that make it a very difficult point to lose in grassy areas. The fingers on the Grasshopper are mounted on a metal ring, enabling the point to be set up as a small game or as a roving point with an accompanying screw-in blunt head. Placing the metal ring behind a Muzzy broadhead can slow down the penetration of the arrow, making it a deadly turkey arrow.

A Target point by Satellite Archery designed for 3-D shooting features easy removal and minimum target damage.

The swamp rabbit is a sporting trophy.

The small game and sport points bowfishing on the Arkansas River.

The Game Nabber from Precision Designed Products is the most recent development. It has what looks like a field point with a jagged flared skirt. The point creates impact and penetration, while the skirt creates hemorrhaging.

Using any of the points at close range requires little if any sight change. For longer distances, though, you may have to hold under or over according to your choice of pins. I prefer a single-pin adjustable sight and often make a few sight markings to accommodate the different types of heads.

Over the years, post-war field archery has been replaced by the 3-D range, while the bowhunting archer has become the most popular form of archery. The bowhunter uses the 3-D range for practicing simply by substituting a field point for a broadhead. 3-D shooting requires the utmost in velocity and a flat trajectory for competition; the screw-in point changes the range from score to game practice. Archers interested in becoming competitive 3-D shooters should opt for the carbonshaft, glue-in target points and either vanes or feathers. ▲

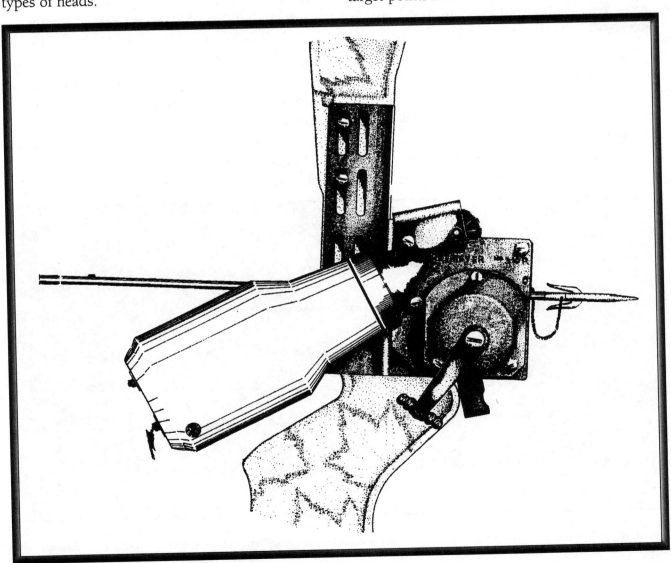

The "Retriever Reel". Courtesy AMS, Inc.

CHAPTER FOURTEEN

The Modern Arrow

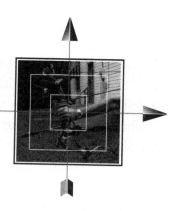

 dvancements in arrow making lagged behind improvements in bow production until the 1930s when Easton perfected the aluminum arrow, replacing wood as the leading shaft material. Since then, makers of fiberglass shafts have tried to displace aluminum as the material of choice but the weight of the fiberglass shaft has hindered its growth.

The manufacture of carbon or graphite arrow shafts began in the 1980s, but production of straight shafts was a problem with early models. When the Beman Company started shipping carbon shafts to the United States in 1989, I frowned on the outsert for broadhead and nock attachment and the light weight for hunting. But colleague Bill Hogue convinced me that an undamaged carbon-graphite arrow served as a good, straight shootable arrow.

Over the last decade, the carbon or graphite shaft has improved with time to produce top-of-the-line arrows. Whether called "carbon" shafts

1. BEMAN ICS—Equipped with a Simmons fieldpoint. • 2. BROWNING GOLD TIP—Equipped with a NAP Spitfire 85 grain expanding broadhead. • 3. EASTON PULTRUDED/CARBON with a Muzzy 4-Blade Glue-on broadhead. • 4. BEMAN HUNTER with NAP Razorbak 100 grain 3-Blade Glue-on broadhead. • 5. EASTON XX75 with NAP 100 grain 3-blade screw-on Thunderhead broadhead. • 6. EASTON XX78 with NAP 125 grain 3-blade screw-on Thunderhead broadhead.

by the Beman Company or referred to as "graphite" shafts by another manufacturer (The Gold Tip Company), these shafts are the preferred choice of many bowhunters today. Beman recently introduced the Internal Component System (ICS) family of shafts, maintaining that the company's production method produces a consistent shaft wall thickness.

Gold Tip shafts have also appeared in the Browning line of archery equipment. They use a slow-setting epoxy to bond the shaft graphite together. Gold Tip adamantly warns bowhunters about not using hot-melt-cement or soaking its shaft in any type of solvent other than a very light wiping with denatured alcohol (a light, fast wipe with a cleaning agent is a good idea when cleaning any brand of carbon or graphite shaft). The Gold Tip seems to bond nicely with any popular brand of fletching cement. Use a #6-32 thread 3/16" Allen set screw to hold nock alignment, remembering that too much pressure can crack an expensive shaft.

Many point inserts and nocks from Easton's XX -75-78 aluminum shafts are interchangeable with both the Beman ICS and Gold Tip models. My feeling is that bowhunters can't go wrong with either of the carbon shafts. The time for aluminum to move over is fast approaching. ▲

Shooting the Oneida Eagle Lite-Force Bow.

CHAPTER FIFTEEN

The Broadhead Arrowpoint

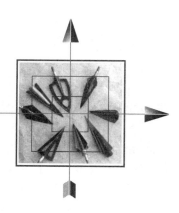

 ost archers are familiar with the types of North American Indian arrow points used centuries ago. Mention native arrow points and the image of a knapped flint point automatically appears. Our country's native archers constructed points of fire-hardened wood, natural glass from lava flows, fish scales, bone and, of course, stone with the right composition to produce a pointed cutting edge.

Thankfully, we modern craftsmen have at our command two types of steel with which to

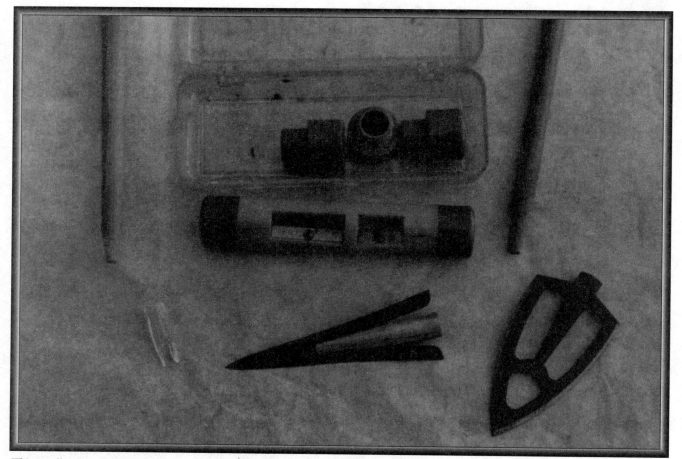

This small taper cutting kit will cut a broadhead and nock taper on any diameter wood arrow shaft. Kit by Saunders, Nock by Bjorn, Broadheads by Howard Hill and the Ben Pearson Deadhead.

Some of the most popular broadheads of the last sixty years. These are the heads that carried us from the thirties to the early eighties. The Hill and the Zwickey are the older. The Rothhaar is the youngest. • 11 o'CLOCK—The Ben Pearson Deadhead. • 1 o'CLOCK—The Bear Razorhead with insert • 3 o'CLOCK—THE MA3. • 5 o'CLOCK—The Hilbre with plastic ferrule and insert. • 6 o'CLOCK—The Replaceable Blade Satellite • 7 o'CLOCK—Roger Rothhaar's Snuffer • 9 o'CLOCK—The Zwickey Black Diamond "Eskimo" • 10 o'CLOCK—The Howard Hill

construct a broadhead arrow point. The most common is a high-carbon steel which is treated to produce an even harder steel, then reheated to relieve the brittleness. Known as cutlery grade steel, it is used to construct most of our top performing two-blade heads.

Stainless steel was originally a stain- and corrosion-resistant construction grade of steel with some uses in the kitchen, such as paring knives and inexpensive grades of tableware. Once it was determined how to raise the carbon content of stainless and classify it as hardened steel, we learned quickly that a blade made from stainless produced a super sharp cutting edge.

Both high-carbon and stainless steel are used in broadhead production these days. A good stainless blade will not lose its edge due to atmospheric moisture. While high-carbon steel blade will produce a better edge, it must be protected with oil, grease or other rust preventative.

Requirements For Broadheads

The ability of a broadhead to retain a sharpened edge is one of the top requirements for a good broadhead. No broadhead is worth having if it causes unusual tuning problems or requires excessive fletching to prevent windplaning. But don't blame a broadhead for being a windplaner until it has been mounted straight on a properly spined shaft equipped with a minimum four-inch helical fletch.

Basic requirements for the broadhead include:

1. *The point must stay together on impact with the animal and remain together upon exiting the animal.*

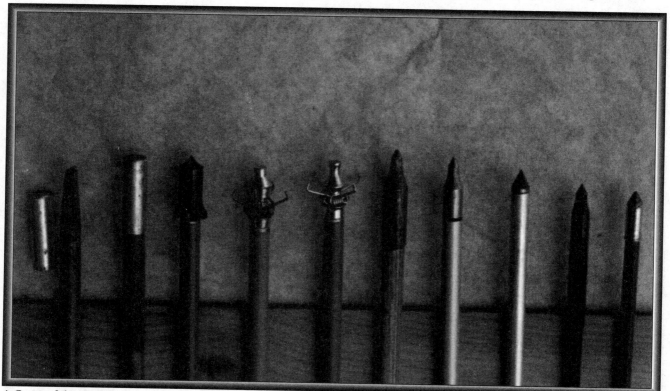

A Group of the sportpoints most commonly shot by today's archers. From left to right • A tapered woodshaft showing the taper hole blunt point separately. • Next to it is the blunt point mounted on a wood shaft. • Third is a new arrival "The Game Nabber". • Fourth is Game Tracker's Shocker 5. • Fifth is the Time Proven Zwickey Judo. • Sixth is a wood shaft taper hole field point. • Seventh an aluminum mounted screw-in field point. • Eighth an aluminum mounted glue-in target point. • Ninth is a screw-in field point mounted on a carbonshaft by use of an outsert. • Tenth is a glue-in target or 3-D point mounted on a carbonshaft

The Satellite Titan Falcon features a fixed stainless broadhead and two auxiliary blades that open on impact. Courtesy Satellite Archery and Seitz Adv.

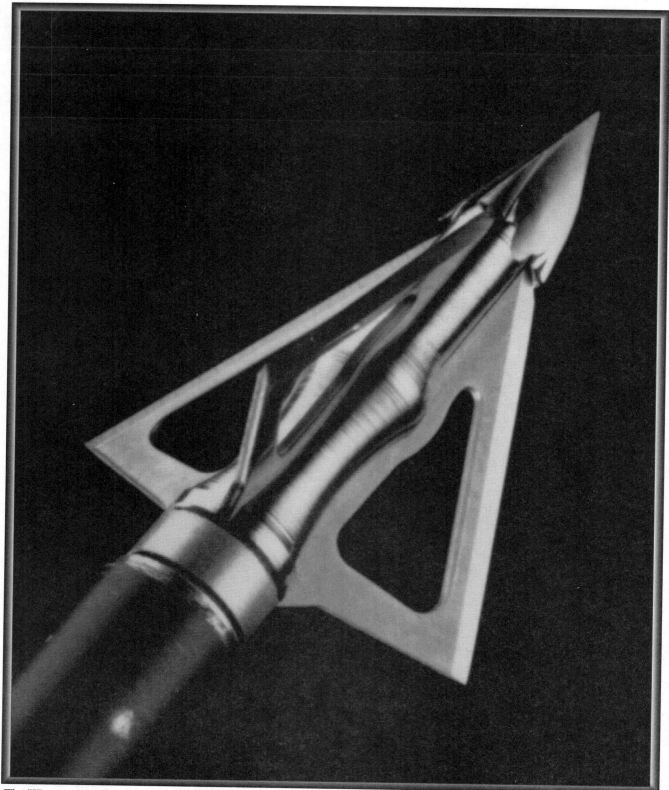

The "Titanium -100" Broadhead body is machined from solid titanium making it one of the strongest broadheads ever made. Courtesy Hawk Assoc. and Barrie Archery.

2. *The point must be sharp on impact and stay sharp all the way through the animal. It should inflict the most hemorrhaging possible and still have enough energy for the arrow to exit the animal.*

3. *The point must must produce good accuracy in order to place the arrow in an animal's vital organs. Any broadhead that comes apart inside an animal should not be tolerated. Once a replaceable blade head starts shedding, the blade stops penetrating. Stopping the arrow means that it no longer causes hemorrhage and has failed to make an exit hole from which to drain the blood.*

Effective Broadheads

Keep the large, two-blade heads on large diameter shafts and shoot them from your favorite recurve. Tip the carbon or thinwall aluminum with multi-bladed, vented heads and opt for speed with your compound. Standard equipment on my hunting arrows are the new Thunderhead and Razorback heads. In over 13 years using Thunderheads, I have seen many a

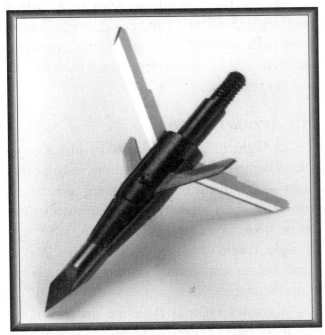

The Satellite Scorpion features four open on impact blades. (Courtesy Satellite Archery and Seitz Adv.)

deer and other game taken with these heads, with only one damaged by a deer.

After learning of the effectiveness of the Muzzy head at the 1994 Arkansas Bowhunter Fall Shoot, I found that the Muzzy also performed well. I've come to realize, therefore, that the two best replaceable broadheads available today are the Thunderhead and the Muzzy. Choose either of these points to tip an arrow shot from a bow suitable in draw weight for the animal being hunted. Place that arrow properly and you can expect complete penetration, short blood trails, and your prize at the end of the short trail.

Recurve Choices

I don't shoot recurves very much anymore because I don't happen to visit those areas where I can shoot the fast-moving, high-flying aerial targets that make for such great fun. My recurve hunting arrows were XX75's tipped with Zwickey Black Diamonds.

Jack Zwickey himself informed me once that his broadhead is the only one still manufactured in its basic form. The early points were hand-made; only updated production has caused a change in appearance.

I have shot the four-bladed Zwickey Deltas and Eskimos from my recurves and they would still be my choice if I had returned to hunting with traditional equipment. Their combination of material, heat treating, and a well-designed, stiff ferrule center section makes an extremely tough broadhead.

Use one of the sharpening tools recommended and you'll have a sharp broadhead with little effort. Always apply a rust protector on high-carbon steel to prevent rusting. Protecting that sharp edge from nicks and quiver dulling is simply good hunting skill. ▲

CHAPTER SIXTEEN

Spine And The Archer's Paradox

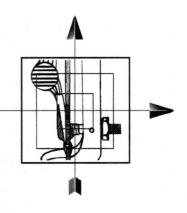

he expression "Straight as an arrow," has been made ever since man began shooting the bow. Yet man has been perplexed over time by the mystery of arrow spine. The earliest archers spent many hours trying to reason why a certain arrow would shoot consistently to the same side of the line of sight.

Man's first solution at controlling spine was to shoot a new arrow and place it with others according to the way they grouped. Arrows that flew straight to the mark were saved for special shots and were known as an archer's "best arrows." The arrows that shot away from the bow were used for occasions when food was plentiful and very little was at stake.

The English were probably the first to develop a mechanical means to measure spine. It was mandatory for a nobleman's archers to gather on the village green every Sunday afternoon for archery practice. Typical targets included a stake, about six feet tall and placed about 100 yards away from the archers. This type of shooting indicated the need for spine control.

The technology that made a "spoked" wagon wheel possible was known throughout western Europe and logically could have been applied to "reive" an arrowshaft from a flat-sided piece of wood. From shaft-making it was relatively simple to compare the stiffness of the shafts, marking another step in the improved accuracy of the bow and arrow.

The wooden tournament-grade arrow produced during the World War II era reached a peak in the control of spine and the physical weight of arrows. The arrival of the aluminum arrow was the first precise control that the "Fletcher" had over a group of arrowshafts. This precise control enabled the "bowyer" to design arrow rests that utilized this uniformity. Arrow rests are available today that eliminate shaft contact at the instant of release. Accuracy becomes dependent on spine and weight control from shaft to shaft. This uniformity duplicates spine flexing and reduces the "arcs of the archer's paradox."

An Arrow's Flight

The flight of an arrow starts by making two arcs. The first arc occurs as the arrow begins its flight — the thrust of the bowstring causing the arrow to make a bend around the arrow rest. The arrow then over-recovers, crossing the line of sight, then swinging back on the line of sight before continuing on a straight course to its target.

An arrow's flight is therefore dependent on the arrow having enough stiffness to make these two arcs without over-controlling. An arrow that

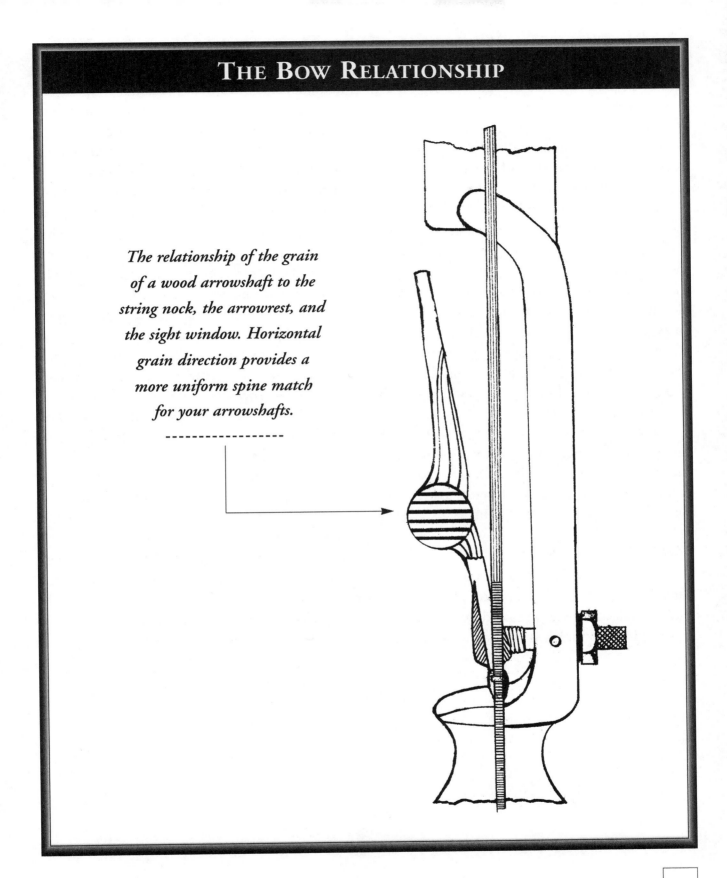

The relationship of the grain of a wood arrowshaft to the string nock, the arrowrest, and the sight window. Horizontal grain direction provides a more uniform spine match for your arrowshafts.

is too stiff will stray too far away on its first arc to return to the line of sight. An arrow that is too weak will cross the line of sight too far on its return to the line of sight.

Fiberglass and the laminated bow have made it possible for the arrow rest to absorb the horizontal and vertical shock once the arrow is released. This has given the archer a means to reduce spine flexing and reduce the "arcs of paradox." The uniformity of arrowshaft material has reduced error from spine variations increased by the action of the finger release. The mechanical release has reduced these two closely related motions to almost zero. [Olympic rules require the recurve and longbow archers to shoot "fingers." Finger shooting will never be as consistent or as smooth as a mechanical release, and this variation calls for a little paradox to help bend the arrow in flight.]

Today's recurve and longbow archers have more problems matching wood arrows because the wood of choice — Port Orford cedar — comes from a narrow strip of forest land on the Oregon coast and is difficult to find.

Variations In Spine

Years ago, a small group of friends and I made early-summer trips to the Pearson Plant in Pine Bluff, Arkansas, where we would buy about 100 unspined and unfinished shafts. We would dip these shafts in lacquer for moisture-proofing and then spine test these shafts for our individual requirements. The small variation in spine and weight of the cedar shaft makes a small amount of paradox an aid to arrow grouping.

The modern centershot compound requires an arrow ranging in spine from stiff to stiffer. The first Beman carbon shafts were rated between 40 and 60 pounds; today's carbon and graphite shafts are rated from 50 to 100 pounds when used with a compound bow. Easton has established a series of spine charts that I use for a number of different types of bows and cams and releases used. Such charts are a good starting point and provide an educational experience for the archer. The modern bow comes already set up with adjustments to meet your draw length requirements. A selection of arrows to match the requirement, plus the help of a professional can easily increase anyone's shooting ability.

A more precise control over spine and weight, coupled with a faster paradox recovery made the aluminum arrow much more accurate for either recurve or compound shooting. The cut-out handle riser and the shoot-through arrow rest, plus the faster paradox recovery of aluminum and carbon shafts, have almost made the "archer's paradox" a thing of the past, thanks to the compound bow and mechanical release. ▲

CHAPTER SEVENTEEN

Arrowshaft Spine Gauge

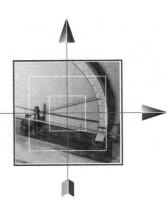

I n days gone by, archers had two or three arrows that they marked and set aside as their "best arrows." These were saved for that special shot when hitting the target meant the difference between meat on the table or preventing some horse thief from stealing your horse.

In the pursuit of producing better arrows, the primitive archer would cut his shafts from a cane thicket each spring, figuring that each piece of cane had roughly the same growth time. After the Civil War, an archer would obtain a plank of cedar, ash or maple and "reive" his shafts from the plank. After reiving the shafts, he would

A commercially built Spine Gauge

DETERMINING FORWARD OF CENTER PERCENTAGES

Suggestion—For ease in mathematics convert your measurements to the decimal system.

Step #1. SHAFT CENTER—*Measure from nock groove to base of point or front of screw-in nsert and mark point equidistant between these two extremes and Name* (**C**).

Step #2. SHAFT BALANCE POINT—*Balance the complete arrow and mark point and name* (**B**).

Step #3. OVERALL SHAFT LENGTH—*Measure from nock groove to base of point or to front of screw-in insert name* (**L**).

Step #4. *Measure distance between points* **C** *and* **B** = 2.8".

Step #5. *Multiply distance between points* **C** *and* **B** *by* **100**.
2.8 *x* 100 = 280

Step #6. *Divide* **280** *by overall shaft length* **26.5"** = **10.5%**. *A* **10%** *Forward of Center is the start of a critical arrow. A* **15%** *Forward of Center is the start of a nosediving arrow.*

May I give credit for this method of calculating FOC to the late Jack Witt who probably obtained it from Easton at least thirty years ago.

check them for straightness and then moisture-proof them. After pointing, nocking and cresting, the arrows were fletched and the fletching trimmed for shape.

When these new arrows were tested for accuracy, some stiff shafts would shoot away from the arrowrest, while weaker shafts shot into the arrowrest. The arrows that flew straight to the mark became the best arrows and were reserved for that "special" shot.

In the early 1900s, some archers began selling their unfinished shafts, offering as well matched spine and moisture-proof shafts at a premium price. These small shops used a simple spine-checking gauge that was self-designed, home-made and easy to build. The return to tradition-al archery and the scarcity of good cedar has brought the importance of a good, simple spine gauge and "homemade" arrows back in favor.

I had always enjoyed making wooden arrows, but like many others I moved on to aluminum, fiberglass and, eventually, carbon arrows for my recurve and longbow shooting. Because these newer materials were all labeled for spine, my spine gauge fell into discard. But the recent demand for wood has made the modern recurve and longbow archers practice with aluminum, saving their "good wood" for competition.

A spine gauge is simple and inexpensive to make. If you are going to "shoot wood," it's a handy gadget to have on hand. The following list describes all the materials needed and explains how to build your own spine gauge.

MATERIALS NEEDED:

- four feet of 1" x 6" board
- one 1/4"-diameter hex head bolt 1-1/2" long
- three 1/4" hex head nuts
- one metal strap 1/8" x 7/8" x 8"
- one piece of carbon arrow shaft 10" to 14" long
- two plastic curtain shaft supports
- one 5" piece of #12 copper wire (solid and uninsulated)
- one large nail that fits inside the carbonshaft
- a short length of wood dowel that fits inside the carbonshaft (to make the indicator tip)
- four 5/8" flat head wood screws
- one screw-threaded metal hook (about 1" hook diameter)
- four 1-1/2" bugle headed screws
- two 3/4" round head screws
- one piece stiff fiberboard or plywood (10" x 12" x 14")
- one piece of slick-finish 10" x 12" cardboard
- small amounts of fletching cement and Devcon five-minute epoxy

(Note: The spine gauge described here is set up for a 28-inch shaft length. This gauge can be adjusted to accommodate a longer or shorter shaft by moving the shaft supports to fit one's needs. Holes must be drilled in the base board to reduce or increase shaft length by one-inch increments. Use the 1-1/2" bugle head screws to make these length adjustments.)

The shaft supports are made of 1" x 6" material cut to 3" wide and 5-1/2" long. The tops of these supports are narrowed to fit the plastic curtain rods that contact the arrowshaft. Attach these supports with small wood screws. The overall length of the wood and plastic support is about 6-1/4" to the bottom of the plastic "V" shaft contact.

The metal strap supports the 1/4" bolt that serves as a rotating shaft for the carbonshaft indicator. The bolt is 6 inches above the base board. Run a drill through one of the nuts, eliminating the threads and allowing the nut to revolve freely around the bolt. Cut a "V" into one flat of this nut and finish it out with a rat tail file, making a contact bed for the epoxy.

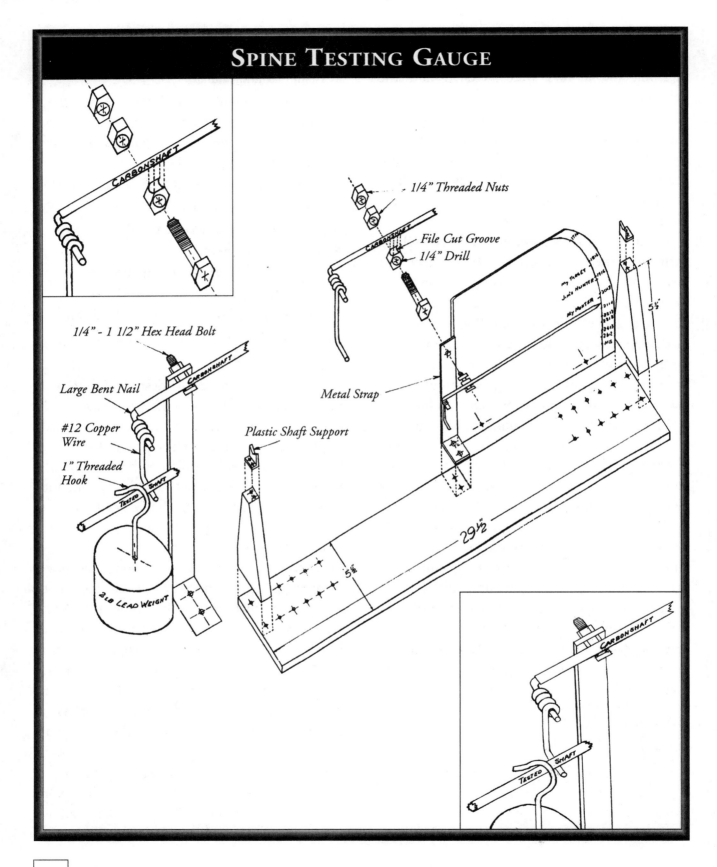

1/4" Threaded Nuts

File Cut Groove

1/4" Drill

5 1/2

Metal Strap

1/4" - 1 1/2" Hex Head Bolt

Large Bent Nail

#12 Copper Wire

1" Threaded Hook

Plastic Shaft Support

29 1/2

5 1/2

2 LB LEAD WEIGHT

CARBONSHAFT

TESTED SHAFT

Bend the large nail into an "L" shape, leaving 7/8" on each leg. Using epoxy, glue the nut to the carbonshaft, allowing for 2 inches from the nut center to the center of the bent nail (after it is inserted and epoxied into the carbonshaft). Check the drawing to clarify the position of the bent nail, the carbonshaft and the hex nut.

Sharpen the small wood dowel and cement it in place on the long end of the carbonshaft. Insert the 1/4" bolt through the nut attached to the carbon indicator and screw it into a threaded nut with enough freedom of movement for the indicator shaft. Now connect the indicator assembly to the vertical shaft with the remaining hex nut.

Check the insert drawing to see how the #12 copper wire is wrapped around the nail about three turns. Now rest a full-length arrowshaft on the plastic shaft supports, making a right-angle bend extending under the arrowshaft. Make adjustments by increasing or decreasing the number of turns until the end of the indicator shaft barely makes contact with the gauge base.

Two pounds works well as a proper weight for spine deflection. You can make a casting for this task with slightly more than two pounds of wheel weights from a tire shop. I used part of an exhausted spray paint can as a mold for my weight. While the lead is still molten, insert the one-inch screw hook.

Make sure there's good ventilation when making this casting, as lead vapor can be hazardous to your health. It will take some time to cool, so be aware of burns. (Note: If your casting is overweight, drill some holes in the casting until the two-pound weight has been reached.)

Your "best arrow" for each bow weight will enable you to set the indicator, gauge the raw shafts, and obtain a matching set of shafts. Look this "best arrow" over to determine the direction of the wood grain, then place that grain in a position vertical to the pull of the spine gauge weight.

When making a spine mark from a painted arrow, grain direction can be determined by placing the string groove of the nock at right angles to the direction of the weight pull. The spine of a woodshaft should be measured with the grain horizontal to the arrowshaft shelf and at 90 degrees to the contact point of the vertical sight window. Mark the arrowspine measurement for the bows in hand. For a wider range of spine markings on your gauge, use some arrows provided by friends.

When shooting aluminum, the first two numbers of the Easton Logo shaft number indicate the shaft diameter in 64th segments of an inch. The last two numbers of the logo serve as the wall thickness measured in thousandths of an inch. The larger the last two numbers, the thicker the shaft wall and the heavier in physical weight of the shaft.

If the sight window permits "in and out" arrowrest adjustment, some additional velocity-cast may be gained by using a lighter weight arrow.　▲

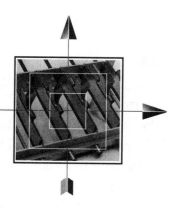

CHAPTER EIGHTEEN

How To Make Your Own Arrows

As you become more deeply entrenched in the sports of bowhunting and 3-D shooting, the desire to make your own arrows will generally ensue. 3-D shooting especially will bring you in contact with other archers who may be shooting home-built arrows. These archers, you may note, can shoot rings around the competition, causing you to wonder: "if you can't beat 'em, then join 'em."

Shooting self-made arrows will not automatically propel you into the winner's circle, but it will provide a continuity in your arrows not attainable in other ways. To get started assembling your own arrows, you'll need to obtain a single helical fletching jig. Look for one that

A Jo Jan Multifletcher Jig. A fine unit for the archer who desires to refletch his arrows in a hurry. This jig is also popular with archery shops to fill custom orders. Courtesy Jo Jan Sportsequip.

provides a choice of fletching configurations. The "Y" fletch — with one feather straight down and the other two feathers set 120 degrees apart — seems to be the most popular setup for 3-D shooting or hunting with a compound bow.

Pick your fletching feathers from the wing that matches your fletching clamp, then plan to stay with that wing choice forever. There is no proven advantage in selecting a right-wing fletch over a left-wing fletch; just remember that you cannot mix right and left wing feathers on the same arrow or use a right wing feather in a left wing clamp (or vice versa). Should you decide to try vanes, your jig and clamp will work fine. Vanes have the advantage of being "ambidextrous" and will work in either right or left clamps.

For your first set of arrows, I recommend a four-inch right wing fletch and a right wing

Trying your adhesive for adherence with carbon shafts

Dipping "masked off" arrow shafts

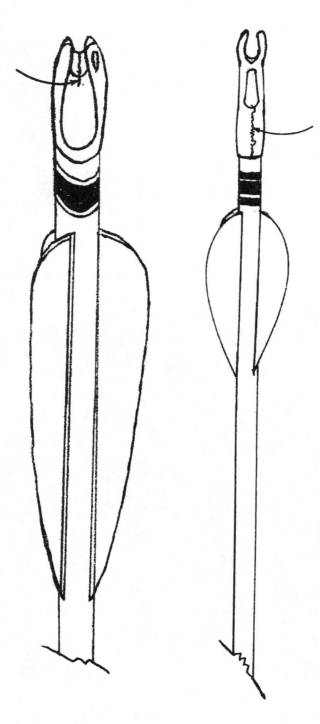

Crack occurring to the griping portion of a slip-on nock. Often caused by glue vapor when too much adhesive is applied as the arrow is fletched. Mounting the fletching too close to the nock is another cause.

Crack in the string seat of a conventional glue-on nock. Too much adhesive at the tip of the shaft nock taper weakens the nock and often causes this damage.

fletching jig and clamp — the sole reason being that these instructions are worded for a right fletch. If you have a left clamp and left feathers, adjust the following instructions accordingly.

Start by sticking a piece of masking tape on the left side of a right helical clamp. Push a nock over a shaft nock taper and set this shaft into the jig. Measure 1-1/4 inches from the center of the nock groove and make a clear mark on the masking tape. Next, measure 4 inches down the clamp and make another mark. These two marks will help determine the fletching clamp offset; they will also increase or decrease the fletching cup drag that controls and prevents windplaning.

Make a centerline down the top of the arrowshaft and set the clamp at a slight angle crossing the centerline halfway between the two marks on the tape. Using a right clamp, move the rear of the clamp 1/32 of an inch to the left of the centerline. Then move the front of the clamp 1/32 of an inch to the right of the centerline and lock the clamp in place. This 1/32 of an inch, plus half the thickness of your clamp, is about the maximum for a large diameter shaft.

Glue the nock in place — being careful to keep the glue away from the smaller area of the nock taper — and fletch the arrow. If your shafts have been cut to length, set the screw-in insert in place with hotmelt and screw a 125-grain field point in place. You now have an aluminum arrow with a lot of cup to your fletch. Find a safe place to shoot and sight in for 35 yards. Without changing sight setting, shoot again with a 100-grain point. Measure the difference in point of impact.

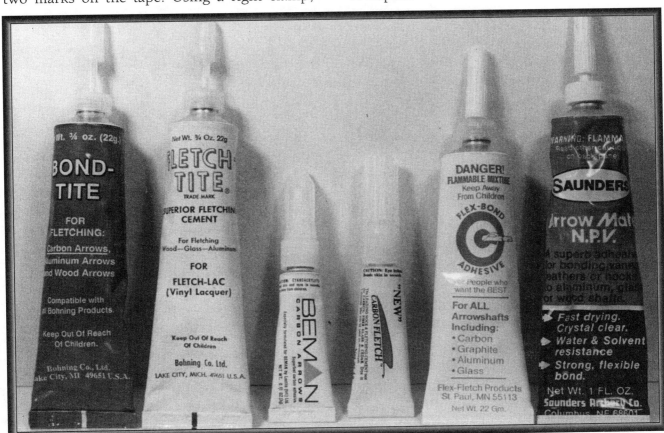

Adhesives used in Fletching arrows

Return home, strip the fletch and reduce the fletching cup by 1/64 of an inch. Go back to the shooting location and, without changing your sight setting, shoot again using both point weights. Record your changes in points of impact. After reducing the fletching cup, I suspect you'll settle for a fletching offset of only 1/32 of an inch on either side of the centerline. This refers, by the way, to the measurement at the base of your fletch, not to the distance to the side of your clamp.

If you intend to shoot broadheads, do not fletch straight down the centerline. You'll create a windplaning arrow unsuitable for dependable shooting. Sometimes a straight fletch will stabilize a light target arrow by using the natural cup of the feather, but don't depend on it without plenty of testing. Study your figures now to see how excess fletching offset can shorten the game-harvesting range of your bow. Your figures on point weight reduction will indicate how this easy second step can add to effective bow range.

New wooden shafts are usually shipped with one or two coats of a clear lacquer sealer. Check the compatibility of the sealer with your cresting lacquers and fletching adhesives. If you have a micrometer, check the diameter of the shaft at each end. You may be surprised to discover that many wood shafts vary a few thousandths of an inch at either end of the shaft. You'll also need a taper cutting tool to make the nock and point tapers. This simple tool, which resembles a hand-turned pencil sharpener, has blades set to cut a 5-degree taper for taper hole points and a 7-1/2-degree taper for the nock end.

This Bitzenerg Fletching Jig has served me and my sons since the early sixties. Naturally my wife's kitchen assisted in arrow production.

INSERT-OUTSERT TOOL
WITH BROADHEAD SHARPENING INSERT

Clearance drill approx. 1/8" deep from rear or insert and screw a 3" x 8-32nds screw thru the rear of the insert. Leave a small gap between screwhead and rear of insert. This small gap increases the holding ability of the epoxy.

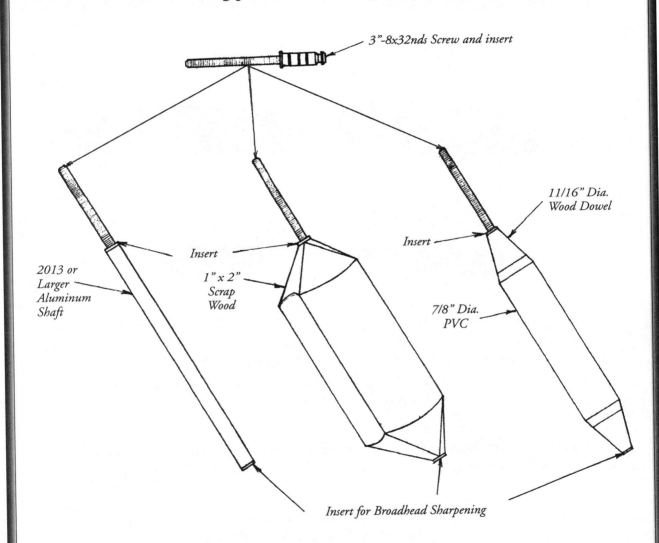

3"-8x32nds Screw and insert

11/16" Dia. Wood Dowel

Insert

Insert

2013 or Larger Aluminum Shaft

1" x 2" Scrap Wood

7/8" Dia. PVC

Insert for Broadhead Sharpening

Use 8x32nds screw end of tool to remove inserts and outserts.
Use insert equipped end of tool to sharpen broadheads equipped with screw-in adaptors.

DETERMINATION OF RIGHT AND LEFT WING FEATHERS

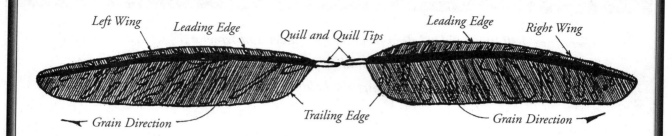

Left Wing   Leading Edge   Quill and Quill Tips   Leading Edge   Right Wing

Grain Direction   Trailing Edge   Grain Direction

Quill has been ground down for installation and shaping

Shield Shape   Parabolic Shape

A barred feather from a mature tom turkey has two distinct colors to it's wing feathers. The outer surface of the feather shows the more brilliant or glossy coloration. The underside is more subdued and is not very visible until the bird is harvested. Place a feather flat with the glossy side up and the grain direction of the trailing edge of the wing feather will give you a clear understanding of just which wing grew that feather.

Modern dyes have both sides of the dyed white feathers just about equal in coloration but feather grain direction will still give you a dependable identification.

The Parabolic Fletch Shape is America's favorite and the more modern fletch shape. Experiments have proved it to produce the quietest flying arrow.

The Shield Fletch Shape is equally comparable to the parabolic for dependable arrow accuracy it is the European archer's favored shape.

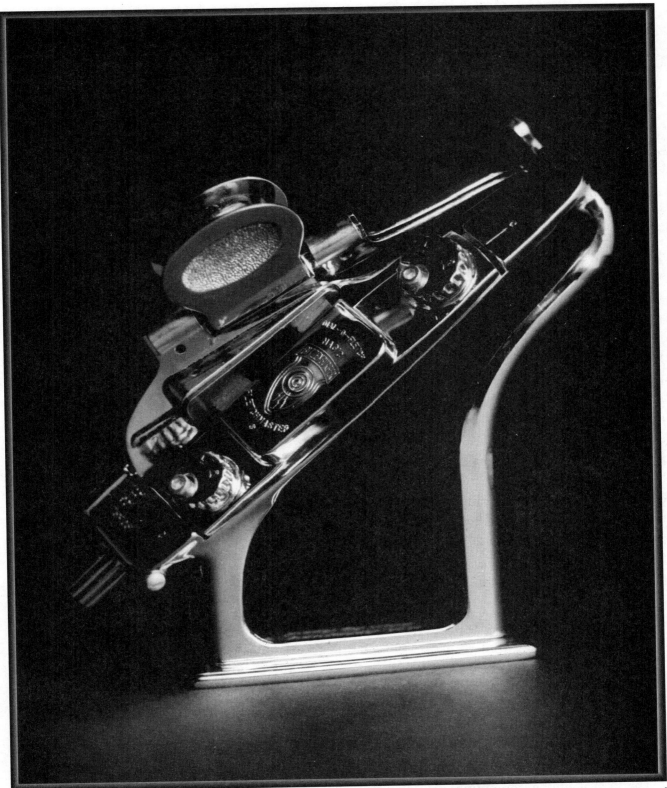

The latest Bitzenburger Fletching tool from a Fletching jig design that was super when first built. The Bitzenburger has fletched uncounted arrows that have won the gold in international competition. Courtesy Bill Anderson of Bitzenburger Machine and Tool Inc.

A selection of inserts adapts the tool for shaft diameters from as small as 7/32-inch diameter to as large as a 3/8-inch diameter. Use the small end of the shaft for the nocks. To determine the draw length for your bow, press on a nock. Now, place a nocked shaft on the bow, hold the bow at full draw, and ask a friend to make a mark even with the back of the bow. Add an additional 3/4-inch plus the length of the point taper. The total of these three lengths represents the true shaft length.

For any taper hole points, use the true shaft length. Cut the shafts to length and then cut the point tapers with the taper cutter. Seal the exposed wood with a thin coat of clear lacquer to prevent moisture absorption. The coating of the nock taper will highlight the wood grain. Always install the nocks with the string groove perpendicular to the wood grain. Uniform nock relationship with the shaft wood grain is another step in spine uniformity among a new set of arrows. Apply the nock adhesive lightly, keeping it away from the small end of the nock taper. Some adhesives can cause the nock to crack in the center of the string groove.

Finally, design the crest allowing 1-1/4 inches from the nock string groove to the back of the fletching. Be sure to allow for the length of the fletching before completing your arrows cresting.

It is tradition for the recurve or longbow to fletch a conventional three-feather fletch with two hen feathers facing the arrowcrest or brushing the side of the bow. The cock feather projects out from the bow. Fifty years ago the fletch standard for broadheads was 5-1/2 inches in length and sometimes exceeding 5/8 inches in height. Little if any offset was used and wind-planing broadheads were common.

The arrival of the compound bow and the thinwall aluminum arrows has made U.S. archers "velocity conscious." The size of the arrow fletching was seen as an obvious factor, so its reduction began. The straight fletch was not dependable for use on a hunting arrow because of windplaning. The offset stopped most of the windplaning, but shortening the fletch length brought back the windplaning problem. My choice is a four-inch, three-feather fletch with a slight amount of helix. I do sometimes get criticized for this choice, but my hunting arrows have proven quite dependable with a very efficient trajectory.

The return to traditional archery has returned "feather burning" to the home workshop. I well remember the days of burning and stinking up the house, causing my wife to descend on me as if I had committed a horrible crime. I built a burner using a transformer with a range of 3 to 12 volts, and bought some nichrome wire from an appliance repair shop (updated feather burners are available in most archery shops these days).

The making and storage of wooden arrows require that you learn how to test a shaft for straightness. Rolling a shaft across a flat surface is one of the simplest but true tests for this. A crooked shaft will produce a "flop-flop" sound. Another method is to support a target- or field-pointed arrow in the palm of your hand and rest the arrow in a vertical position. Blow across the fletching, making the arrow spin. A straight arrow will spin very rapidly.

Every bowhunter needs two storage containers for his arrows. One should be a large container capable of holding several dozen arrows for permanent storage. The other should be a smaller, portable case that will hold and protect 12 to 18 arrows during transport.

It's a good idea to build some inexpensive storage boxes from plywood (see drawings in this chapter). Wood arrows will warp if left leaning against a corner of a closet, and moths will feast on them, causing refletching — and a bad disposition on your part.

Carbon shafts will absorb cleaning agents and destroy the cresting and fletching, so be sure that when dipping a short length of carbonshaft the nock end of the shaft is plugged up with a wooden dowel. Also, mask off a short distance past where the screw-on or slipover will reach. Do not apply lacquer where the nocks fit, and don't apply adhesive to hold the nock in place. Buy an Easton nock tool to attach and adjust the nocks. Determine the carbon shaft length and cut your shafts to the proper length to complete your arrows.

Carbonshaft cutting should only be done with a high-speed cutoff wheel. Whether you're cutting one or a thousand carbonshafts, wear a mask before microscopic dust from the shaft can settle into your lungs.

A fine adhesive developed especially for the carbonshaft is Bohning's STIK-TITE. It is superior to the fast-setting epoxies because it can be applied or loosened at lower temperatures. Taking safety precautions to avoid the danger of using electrical soldering irons near water, quench the point (or outset) with water when it is seated.

For a permanent installation use Devcon 5-Minute Epoxy. Do not apply any flames around the shaft area. The faster an epoxy settles, the lower temperature required for it to soften.   ▲

A young feather burner showing a shaped burner ribbon in place and a unshaped ribbon at the base of the unit.

CHAPTER NINETEEN

Cleaning Arrowshafts

 hen cleaning arrow shafts, hunters should follow some basic rules to protect the shafts and themselves while handling cleaning agents. First, always wear protection — such as a good pair of latex gloves — when cleaning shafts and handling lacquer, isopropyl alcohol or other volatile cleaning agents. Second, clean carbon-shafts one at a time, using a thinner compatible with the cresting and fletching agents used. Isopropyl alcohol 91% works well when combined with a thorough drying.

Thinners and cleaning agents used in cleaning shafts, fletching and cresting arrows

Give the carbonshaft a light wiping with a paper towel barely moistened with the cleaning agent. Then swish the freshly-wiped shaft through the air several times. That will keep the agent from being absorbed by the carbonshaft. Holding the shaft close to a light bulb, warm the shaft until, when touching the shaft to your cheek, a warm feeling is produced. Overheating will damage the carbonshaft.

Do not attempt to dip carbonshafts — either individually or in a bunch — into the cleaning agent. Once trapped inside the shaft, these cleaning agents can gradually penetrate the shaft wall and lift the cresting and fletching off the shaft. It's like peeling the skin off a banana.

Wood shafts require application of a moisture-proof agent to keep the shaft from absorbing moisture during storage or in ground contact while shooting. Check for compatibility of your dipping lacquer with the fletching, nocking and cresting chemicals. Moisten a paper towel with a thinner and give each shaft a light wiping. Keep wearing gloves until the dipping is complete.

Aluminum shafts can be cleaned and degreased easily with a paper towel moistened with thinner. The cleaning process is meant simply to remove finger grease deposited while handling. Do not moisten the area around the XX78 Super Slam UNI bushing, which is installed by an adhesive that may be loosened by excessive amounts of shaft cleaner.

The latest technology in arrowshaft materials, the carbon shaft absorbs excess cleaning agents and soaks up natural grease from fingertips. Mold release agents can ruin a good-looking crest job and cause poor adherence for fletching. Wear latex gloves until the cleaning and cresting are complete.

Archery shops also carry MEKs — methyl ethyl keytones — as cleaning agents. In the pure state, MEKs can penetrate certain types of latex gloves and then be absorbed into one's internal system, even affecting internal organs. Several other cleaning agents can be used in place of MEKs without risk. If you have used any MEKs, check with the Department of Pollution and Ecology in your state for proper disposal instructions. ▲

CHAPTER TWENTY

Selecting The Nocks

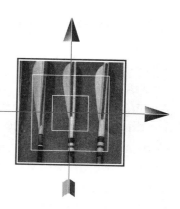

The proper selection and installation of nocks is another important step in the production of an efficient arrow. The following descriptions cover the different types of nocks available, along with their specifications and the shafts that accommodate them.

The Easton XX75 utilizes the conventional machined nock taper set at 7-1/2 degrees. A large number of companies make nocks to this taper specification (and, unfortunately, to their own plastic formulation). Be aware of chemical incompatibility between the nock and the adhesive being used. Keep the adhesive away from the inside of the string groove, and do not dip or paint the nock taper. Check for accuracy of nock alignment with a gauge, or by test-shooting the new arrows and watching for signs of unusual flight or inaccuracies. Remove damaged nocks by gently twisting with pliers while applying heat. This shaft may have to be changed to the UNI bushing and Super Nock arrangement. The XX78 Super Slam utilizes a factory-installed UNI bushing and a Super Nock with a straight-sided projection to screw into the bushing. Use an Easton nock tool to seat and align the super nock. Avoid the use of adhesives.

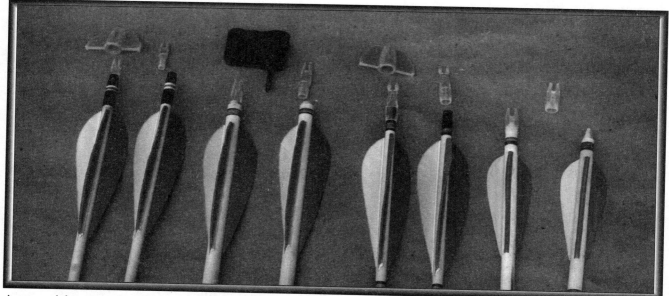

Arrows and the new nocks to fit them. (From left to right in pairs) • FIRST PAIR—The Pultruded/Carbon equipped with an outsert • SECOND PAIR—The XX78 and the Super Uni Bushing • THIRD PAIR—The Beman Hunter with the slip-over nock Adhesive is not recommended for nock installation for the above mentioned nocks. • FOURTH PAIR—The XX75 with the nock taper. Adhesive is required for this nock.

To remove a damaged nock, backit out with a nock tool or pliers. Remove the damaged UNI bushing by inserting a wood screw into the bushing, applying heat, then pulling until the bushing comes out. Remember, too much heat can damage the molecular structure of an aluminum shaft. After lightly sanding the inside of the shaft, a new UNI bushing can be put in as a replacement with Devcon 5-minute epoxy.

The Beman Hunter Carbonshaft uses a slipover nock. Set this nock in place with an Easton nock tool as the nock is pushed and twisted in place (an adhesive is not recommended).

The Easton Pultruded Carbonshaft provides a choice of a slipover pultruded/carbon nock or a nock outsert matched with the Easton aluminum/carbon Extreme nock, which is smaller in size than a Super Slam Super Nock.

Do not use adhesives when installing a slipover nock., After a mild sanding and cleaning, install the nock outsert using Devcon's 5-minute epoxy. Remove damaged nocks with wood screws, applying heat while pulling on the screw.

Should the nock taper insert be damaged, it can be pulled out by applying heat with a high-wattage soldering iron. After pulling the nock taper, install a new nock insert with Devcon 5-minute epoxy or Bohning STIK-TITE hot melt. Apply a twisting motion as set-up occurs.

The wooden arrow has always been one of archery's big challenges, simply because an off-center or misaligned string groove can affect its accuracy.

The modern wooden arrow uses a plastic nock, commonly found in most archery shops. The nock taper is cut by a small hand tool forming a 7-1/2 degree taper for the nock and a 5-degree taper for the taperhole arrowpoints. The grain line of a wood arrow is placed horizontal to the arrow rest. The nock is always glued in place with the string groove perpendicular to the grain line. Uniform positioning of the grain line in relation to the arrow rest helps control spine paradox and produces a more uniform grouping from a set of arrows.

Fletch Tite is not recommended for attaching nocks because this adhesive melts many of the plastic nocks available. When using Fletch Tite for fletching, until the Bjorn nock came along, we had to use cement other than FletchTite for the nocks. Early models of the Bjorn nock seemed a luxury, with its accurately built-in snapnock features and an ability to be glued in with Fletch Tite. The modern Bjorn nock is still available and remains popular wherever the nock taper is used for either wood or aluminum.

Every manufacturer of carbon shafts seems to have produced their own nock systems, with some having been duplicated by independent suppliers. Most of these nocks do not use an adhesive. The early plastic nocks had a flat surface at the bottom of the string groove. Newer models, however, have a well-rounded groove at the bottom of the nock. This arrangement seems to complement the very short bows and sharp string angles that occur at full draw. These new systems work well, performing more accurately than any nock system known to date. ▲

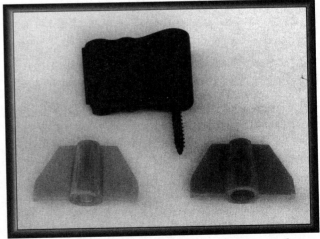

Tools produced by Easton to install, adjust and remove the new designed arrownocks. The screw projecting from the top tool will help remove a damaged nock from the XX78 Super Uni Bushing. The two bottom tools help install and align with the fletching only.

CHAPTER TWENTY-ONE

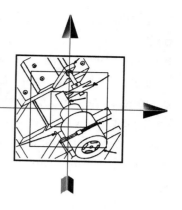

Arrow Cresting

he main purpose for painting or decorating an arrow has always been to serve as a means of identification for archers. In ancient times an arrow's markings made it simple to identify which archer struck an arrow into an enemy soldier and which one saved the village during enemy attack.

On Sunday afternoons, when every able-bodied man had to report to the village green for archery practice, the crested arrow highlighted the best shot of that day's contest, leaving no room for argument about the top shooter for that afternoon.

Years ago, many archery shops would register customers' crests for duplication whenever they ordered arrows. Dipping the wooden shaft was necessary to seal out moisture and reduce warpage, but with the arrival of aluminum, shaft dipping diminished. The National Target Association still requires some identification on a competitor's arrows, but I know of only one archery shop in Arkansas that advertises dipped and crested arrows.

Each archer has a preference for the color of his arrow and its markings. Hill, Bear and Pearson all used white-shafted arrows because they showed up against most natural backgrounds for photographic purposes. I prefer a "bright arrow" for hunting and target, since it

is remains visible while in flight and helps prevent shooters from developing the bad habit of "peeping," or watching the arrow on its way to the target. These bright arrows also clearly pinpoint arrow impact; it's also easy to spot them sticking in the ground after they've passed through a game animal.

A dark arrow can disappear against a natural background the instant it's shot. This vanishing arrow doesn't tell you anything about the shot unless you can find either the entry wound on the animal, the arrow itself, or an immediate blood trail.

These distinctions explain how a bright crested arrow earns its place in your quiver and pays well for its keep.

For archers who want to complete the cresting task on their own, here are a number of tips on the arrow cresting process and the setup, materials and steps involved. The drawing of the home-built cresting machine included in this chapter (see page 113) will also provide assistance. Most dipping calls for a short dip tube to cover aluminum or carbon shafts from the nock taper to the shaft logo. Since the wood shaft must be moisture-proofed so it won't become a warping nightmare, a full-length tube is required to cover the shaft, nock taper and point taper.

You'll need to construct a cresting machine to rotate the arrow shaft as the decorative lacquer is

A Homemade Arrowshaft Cresting Machine

FIGURING CRESTING SHAFT SPEED

Motor Drive Pulley: 0.875 *(Dia.)* x 3.14 *(Pi.)* x 625 *(RPM)* = 1719 Inches

2.00" Vee Pulley: 3.14 *(Pi.)* x 2.00 *(Dia.)* = 6.28 Circumference

1719/6.28 = 274 RPM Cresting Shaft Speed

This is a sketch of a homemade cresting machine that I made years ago. All wood components are 1" x 6" pine. The motor came from a broken sewing machine purchased very inexpensively at a carport sale. The short pillar block was modified by adding a longer shaft.

If you have some scrap parts and mechanical ability this sketch may help.

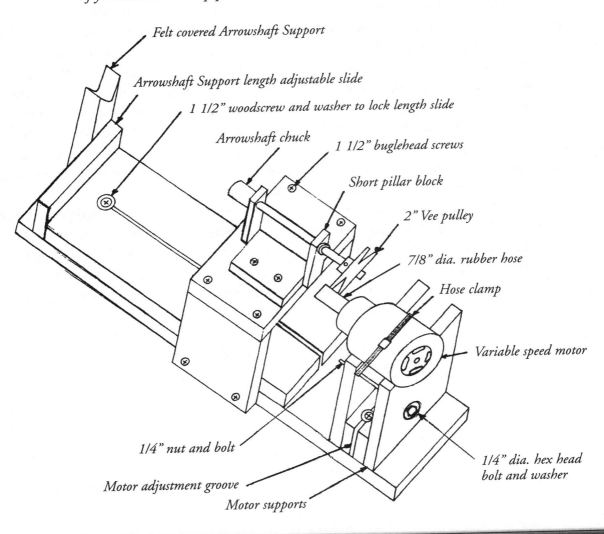

Felt covered Arrowshaft Support

Arrowshaft Support length adjustable slide

1 1/2" woodscrew and washer to lock length slide

Arrowshaft chuck

1 1/2" buglehead screws

Short pillar block

2" Vee pulley

7/8" dia. rubber hose

Hose clamp

Variable speed motor

1/4" dia. hex head bolt and washer

1/4" nut and bolt

Motor adjustment groove

Motor supports

applied. Drill presses set to the lowest rpm work well when the shaft is contained between two felt pads to eliminate vibration. This setup can be used when working in a vertical position and only a few arrows are being crested.

I found a small, variable-speed motor at a carport sale and it has powered a home-built cresting machine for many years. A five-inch pulley rotated by a piece of rubber tubing inserted over the motor drive was used to reduce the rpm's of the machine. To eliminate vibration, the pulley was also attached to the end of a pillar block shaft.

The arrowshaft chuck was made from a piece of thick-walled rubber tubing placed over the end of the pillar block shaft. A piece of PVC was then pushed over the tubing. The felt-covered arrowshaft support, which is adjustable for length, helps smooth out the shaft's rotation (I try to rotate the arrowshaft at around 300 rpm).

Quality brushes should be used for cresting. Cheaper brushes will shed a hair when least desired and can ruin your work. Start with brushes of 1/8-inch width and 1/16th-inch widths. Add a third brush with a small width to cap off the larger paint bands and give your cresting a professional look. You can add to this selection of brushes as skill and experience increase.

Cresting lacquers come in one-ounce jars in a variety of colors. I prefer Bohning lacquers, thinners and adhesives because they are all compatible and are generally available at most archery dealers. You'll also need a small container to hold the cleaning thinners and materials and several paper towels for drying.

Shafts should be hung vertically to dry (shafts laid horizontally are likely to collect globules of lacquer on the underside of the shaft). If you prefer lacquer on the thin side, add several drops of thinner when cresting has been completed, prior to closing the containers.

Some professional cresters like the shaft to rotate towards them. The wet lacquer is applied as it rotates under the shaft, offering a better view of the work as it spins over the shaft towards them. Others prefer working on the shaft as it rotates away from them. After trying both ways, I decided that a good hand rest while doing this work was more important than shaft direction.

I recently priced the materials necessary to put together this cresting home workshop and was surprised they could be ordered or the equipment obtained in kit form a lot cheaper than I could buy the separate components. ▲

CHAPTER TWENTY-TWO

The Broadhead Collector

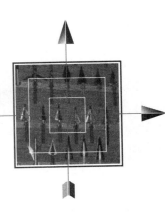

Someone once stated that there has been more time devoted to designing arrows and arrow points than in the design of the modern day jet fighter. This would explain the popularity of collecting arrowheads among sportsmen, and the origin of a club for such collectors. The American Broadhead Collectors Club was founded in 1974 and today has more than 130 active members from all over the globe. Members are continually on the lookout for broadheads to add to their collections.

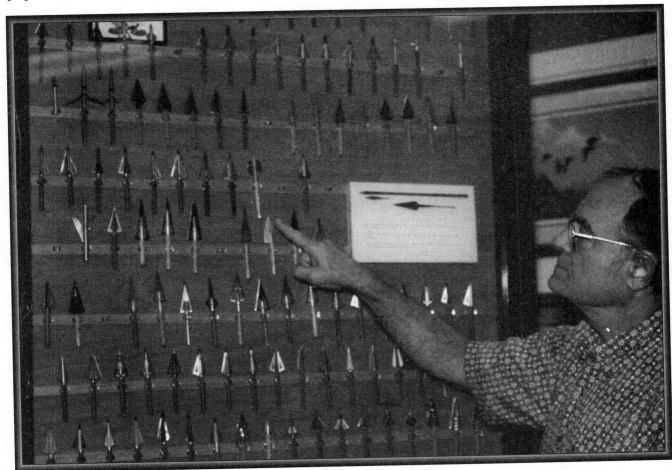

Larry Guinn points out a Pioneer Game Tamer in his broadhead collection.

This "hobby within a hobby" seem to take great pride in showing off its past while pointing a path to the future, as club members go to great lengths to display their arrowheads. Tournaments and other gatherings, such as the Ben Pearson Memorial Tournament, regularly feature one or more collectors.

Club Director Larry Guinn became involved in the mid-'80s after seeing the collection of a friend. His own collection has grown to over 1,300 on display, with many more awaiting construction of display cases. Among the sources of Larry's broadheads are the customers who visit his archery shop, Hunter's Choice. Larry believes that you're not a serious collector until you own a point known as the "Pioneer Game Tamer," which resembles a field point with a rotating sharpened disk mounted lengthwise in the rear portion of the ferrule. The designer of this point wanted this circular disk blade to roll over any bone that it hit.

Broadhead collecting rapidly spread into other types of points used in archery. The only type of point not considered is the stone point. Many club members acquire stone points but the group considers them as one-of-a-kind arrow points. The Broadhead Collectors Club has an elected slate of officers and publishes a newsletter four times each year. The group also keeps a listing detailing the description and history of commercially manufactured broadheads. Interested readers can learn more about the group by contacting: Mr. Joe Lange, Membership Chairman, 703 W. Carol St., Colby, WI 54421; (715) 223-2537. ▲

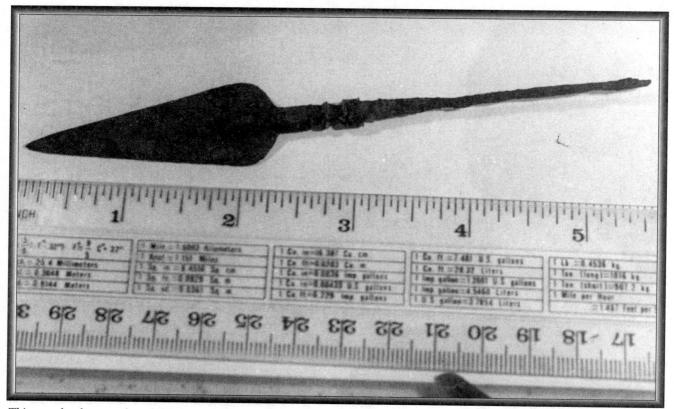

This arrowhead was made and shot by one of Attila's Huns about 450 A.D.

CHAPTER TWENTY-THREE

Some Bowstring History

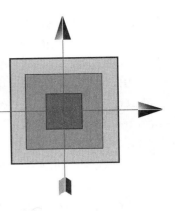

 hen primitive man made the first bow, it's probably because he had discovered how to shoot a short shaft from the same bow he used to rotate a fire drill, or he had learned how to rotate a fire drill from the bow he used for shooing arrows. However it happened, the first bowstring was probably made of rawhide, no matter where that first bow was shot. And I'll wager that early man didn't shoot many arrows until he started the search for a better bowstring. Animal matter was too handy at the time, so sinew probably became the first improved bowstring. Linen and hemp were later used, with hemp outperforming all other grown material. Hemp lasted until after World War II, when dacron became available. From that day forward chemistry, not Mother Nature, produced our bowstring material.

The reason anyone seriously considers making his own bowstrings is improved performance — and much of a bow's performance depends on a good string. Fortunately, the days of poor-quality factory strings are behind us; I haven't seen a factory string fail because of poor construction in several years.

The first thing to do after acquiring a new bow is to match your nocking point diameter to the nock groove size of your arrows. This chapter will explain how to perform this simple check and how to correct the problem (if there is one).

Competitive recurve archers are the most attentive to bowstring problems. They generally shoot according to Olympic rules without using a string peep, or a mechanical release, and with no let off while aiming at full draw. The York Round at 90 meters will weed out the master archers from the arrow shooters in a hurry. You can bet these archers make their own bowstrings — or have them made to their exact specifications.

When it comes to worrying about arrow flight, the 3-D shooters take the cake. I have often seen small arrow nocks jammed on large diameter string servings. One slight bit of attention to matching string groove size to string serving diameter will pay big dividends in better arrow flight and increased arrow cast or velocity.

When I began stringmaking to supply the competitive needs of two of my sons, I used the original dacron material of varying strength and stretch characteristics. Dacron B-50 was one of the early string material improvements, and it served well through the development of fiberglass and the wood-laminated bow and on up to the present day.

The cushioning effect of B-50 on bowlimbs as an arrow is launched and the limbs return to brace height helps prevent the limbs from delaminating. Don't use those recently introduced super-strength, no-stretch materials to make a string for older recurves and longbows. And don't even think about it with newer recurves, longbows and some of the compounds unless the manufacturer approves it. Brownell's Sports Products (Moodus, Conn.) supplied America's archers with bowstring materials until BCY Inc. entered the market. I like the way BCY states the approved use for each of its string materials.

Be safe and use the string material recommended by the bow maker, but if this information is not available go with the information supplied by whoever makes the string material, because it can prevent damage to a treasured bow.

The arrival of the super-strength, low stretch fibers, starting with Fast Flight, initiated a major design change in compound design. Elimination of the teardrops and steel cables, then going directly to string posts or the cams, have produced another increase in arrow velocity. Material such as Spectra and several other registered trade names stir one's curiosity as to just which superfiber the new one-cam bows will use. Will it be specifically named Spectra, or another simply referred to as a synthetic polymer.

Getting started in string making is not expensive — provided you make your own jig. The one shown in this section is very basic and can be made with simple home tools. It will duplicate factory-made jigs, plus the extension can be removed and stored until needed. This jig can be constructed for less than $25, which is considerably less than the cost of a factory jig. The serving tools are inexpensive, too, generally about $5 each. Buying two of these serving tools will, in fact, save time and money; they are also assets when it comes to controlling tension on the serving material.

The cost of conventional Dacron B-50 or B-500 is quite reasonable, with 1/4 pound enough to make several strings for a recurve or a longbow. I have not seen a price list for the two string materials BCY recommends for teardrop-equipped compounds, but I suspect they are reasonable.

Should you decide on using Fast Flight or more sophisticated fiber, then costs will increase. Buying a bowstring made from a superfiber could cost $30, which justifies the purchase of 1/4 pound of Fast Flight or StreamLINE.

Some comments on stringmaking:

✦ *The string-making jig described here is expandable, inexpensive, easy to build and will serve the home archer and the professional shop well. One serving tool is necessary, but two are much more convenient. Serving tools are inexpensive and available at most archery shops.*

✦ *Empty spools for holding a variety of monofilament center servings may be hard to find; try inquiring at a local shoe repair or tailor shop.*

✦ *Small diameter serving cord seems to do better on campost loops and teardrop attachments. Recurves and longbows seem to prefer a larger-diameter cord depending on the strand count in the bowstring.*

✦ *Use medium tension with cord and monofilament servings — and never use monofilament on a bowstring's ends or loops.*

✦ *Bow string wax should be applied before installing any string accessories. Burnish wax into the string with a small piece of folded leather. BCY makes a special synthetic wax — called ML6 — for its line of bowstring material. Bohning makes Tex-Tite string wax for early dacron-synthetic string material and Seal-Tite, a silicone-based wax, for the new high-tensile strength string materials. Stay with the old beeswax for the Flemish Twist strings.*

In covering the even numbered strings (12-14-16, etc.), I haven't mentioned the odd-strand string. The new bowstring materials are much stronger, and the new synthetic string waxes are so much slicker, that the old waxes and odd-strand bowstrings are just plain obsolete. The new materials provide a stronger, lighter, more durable and more dependable bowstring. ▲

CHAPTER TWENTY-FOUR

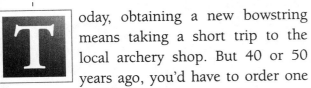

An Expandable String Jig

Today, obtaining a new bowstring means taking a short trip to the local archery shop. But 40 or 50 years ago, you'd have to order one from a sporting goods store. Spare bowstrings and other archery equipment were not stock items in sporting goods stores, while getting a bowstring from the factory could mean a six-week wait.

Necessity has been called the mother of invention. Years ago, when a hunting partner needed a new bowstring, I fastened together a homemade string jig with two tenpenny finishing nails and a piece of two-by-four pine. The Boy Scout manual recommended linen for bowstrings, so a friendly shoemaker came to the rescue with some material. By using only a small amount of ingenuity, my friend had his bow shooting again — but its creation left much to be desired. It was some time later before we had spare factory-built string. Tournament archery demonstrated that a handcrafted string offered some real advantages over factory-built string. With increased arrow speed and better flight delivering real dividends, I decided to build my first string jig. It was very simple, served well for recurves, and lasted into the day of the compound. The arrival of the new superfibers and the elimination of steel cables on the recently-designed compounds made my old jig

obsolete in a hurry. Some modern bows require strings over 95 inches in length, so my old jig will require some redesigning.

A local archer once built a conventional short jig using a material found in the electrical construction field called "Unistrut." Few people, including many professional shops, have enough room to use and store a ten-foot string jig. I think that the solution described here is simple and quite reasonable in cost. Refer to the list of materials on (page to come) featuring the expanded drawing. The piece of Unistrut is available at most electrical supply houses and comes in ten-foot lengths. Get the 1 5/8-inch size with elongated, perforated holes in the bottom side.

Then, with a hacksaw, cut the Unistrut into one 6-foot piece and one 4-foot piece. Taking two Unistrut clamps, remove the springs and note the 3/8-inch by 16 threaded holes. The two clamps fit under the rolled edge of the Unistrut and provide for easy adjustment of the stringpost brackets. Note that the common hole size is 3/8 inches (except for the four 1/2-inch diameter stringpost holes). The 2-inch x 1/4-inch x 14-inch flat stock may be obtained at a local welding shop. You may already have the short two-by-fours that make the mounting pads, and a trip to a hardware store will provide the nuts, bolts, wing nuts

AN EXPANDABLE STRING JIG

REQUIRED MATERIALS

10' – 1 5/8" Perforated Unistrut
2 Pieces – 2" x 4" x 16" Pine
2 Pieces – 2" x 1/4" x 14" Flat Stock
4 Bolts – 1/2" x 13thds x 7"
8 Hex Head Nuts – 1/2" x 13thds
2 Stove Bolts – 3/8" x 16thds x 2"

2 Wing Nuts – 3/8" x 16thds
4 Stove Bolts – 3/8" x 16thds x 1"
2 Hex Head Bolts – 3/8" x 16thds x 1"
6 Hex Nuts – 3/8" x 16thds
2 Flat Washers – 3/8" Dia.

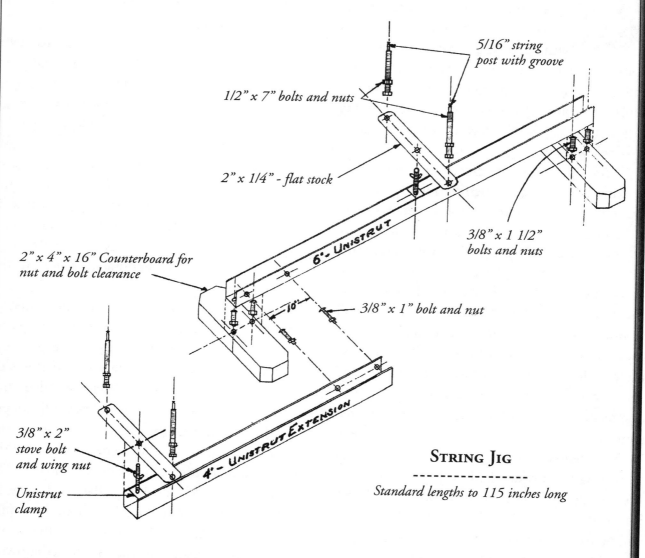

5/16" string post with groove

1/2" x 7" bolts and nuts

2" x 1/4" - flat stock

3/8" x 1 1/2" bolts and nuts

2" x 4" x 16" Counterboard for nut and bolt clearance

6'- UNISTRUT

3/8" x 1" bolt and nut

4' - UNISTRUT EXTENSION

3/8" x 2" stove bolt and wing nut

Unistrut clamp

STRING JIG

Standard lengths to 115 inches long

and washers required. The can of spray paint is optional.

There may be minor problems in making the string posts and lining up the hole so the two pieces of Unistrut can be bolted together. Drill two holes the diameter of a short nail in one piece of Unistrut on ten-inch centers. Grind a sharp point on the tip of the nail. Clamp the Unistrut pieces together with a "C" clamp. Insert the pointed nail through the small holes, making a small mark on the painted surface of the opposite Unistrut. Now centerpunch and drill two 3/8-inch holes.

The stringposts are made by cutting the hex heads from each of four 7-inch bolts with a hacksaw. Polish these cuts. Reduce the diameter of the severed bolt ends to 5/16-inch diameter with a grinding wheel and a flat file. Make these diameter reductions about one inch in length. The string post caps on most compound cams are about 5/16-inch in diameter.

Use a small, round file to cut a groove about 1/16-inch deep. Making this grooved cut will leave a one-inch long 5/16-inch diameter post with a 3/16-inch diameter string groove at the opposite end of the original 7-inch threaded bolt. Two washers and nuts are required to attach each string post bracket to the flatstock bracket. The wingnuts will secure the string post brackets to the Unistrut clamps, providing easy length and angle adjustments.

You now have a conventional-length jig for the older compounds, the recurves and the longer longbows. Attach the extension and move one string post bracket; you can now make the super-length strings for the new one-cam bows. If you ever need the super-length feature, remember that bowhunters are prone to move up to the latest high-performance hunting bows, which means you'd need a spare super-length string.   ▲

CHAPTER TWENTY-FIVE

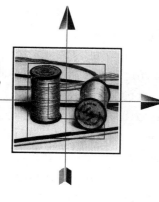

Making A Continuous Loop Bowstring

This chapter outlines the process of creating a continuous loop bowstring. It includes tips on selecting the string material needed, the tools needed to complete the project, and the steps required to manufacture the bowstring.

Step 1:

Set up your basic tools: a string jig, two serving tools, a sharp knife, a tape measure, lacquer thinner, string wax of the correct type, Stern Lok-Knot adhesive, a piece of 1-inch x 3-inch leather, and a black Sharpie pen.

450 PREMIUM - a new super fiber used in making bowstrings. Courtesy BCI Inc.

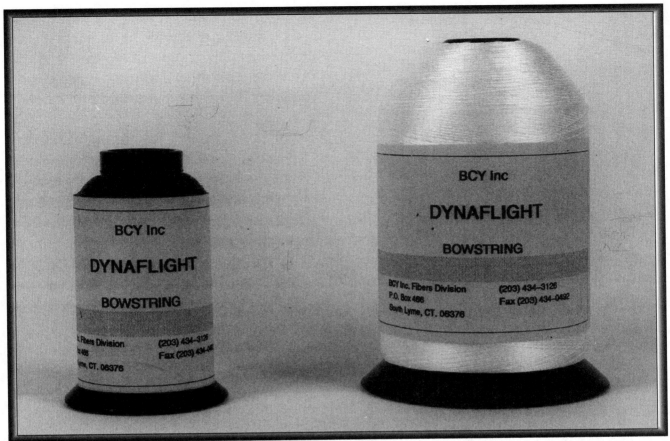

DYNAFLIGHT - a new super fiber used in making bowstrings. Courtesy BCI Inc.

Step 2:

Determine the string material needed. For a recurve or longbow stay with B-50 or B-500 unless the bowmaker states otherwise. For a teardrop compound follow BCY's recommendation with 450 Premium or try DynaFLIGHT.

If a superlength string is needed for the new one-cam bows, most archery shops will carry a spool of Fast Flight. I know of an emergency string made of Fast Flight for a bow with unidentified string material that has been shooting for four months. The coming years will create so much demand for the superfibers that most archery shops will stock several brands.

When possible, stay with the material recommended by the bowmaker (if identifiable).

Step 3:

Obtain the string loop serving material. Your local archery shop can supply a cord material made specifically for loop serving and may even supply a choice of colors and diameters. DO NOT USE a monofilament material for loop end serving. Monofilament can act as a sanding agent on teardrops or camposts. Its action can remove the finish from recurve or longbow string grooves, allowing moisture to enter and swell the tip laminates, causing major damage.

Step 4:

Compare the strands used in the factory-equipped string with the recommendation for draw weight from the fiber manufacturer.

Often times bow makers tend to go heavy and use more strands than necessary.

Step 5:

Determine string length. Check the bow specification chart attached to the inside lower limb. Give this figure preference over measuring the old string, which may be longer than specifications require because the length increases due to length increase as it's used. Experience will sometimes indicate a 3/8-inch to 1/2-inch shorter distance called for between jig string posts to allow for an anticipated stretch in length as the string is used. Comparing the length of the old string against length specifications can provide an estimate of how much stretching is possible. Line up your string posts with the length of the jig. Measure string length from the outside extremities of the string posts.

Step 6:

Wrap the required number of strands of string material around the two extreme string posts, allowing about 8 inches on each end of the open strands to tie the loopknot.

Pull the loose ends tight and, at a point equi-distant from the ends of the loose strand,

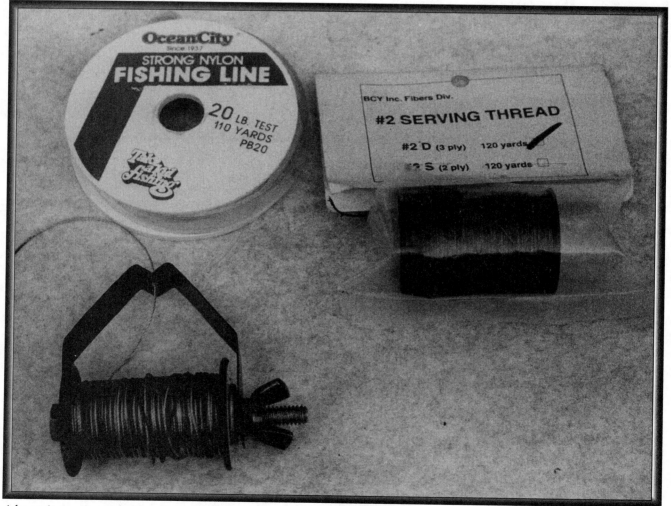

A bowstring serving tool with nylon monofilament for your center serving and fabric thread for bowstring loops.

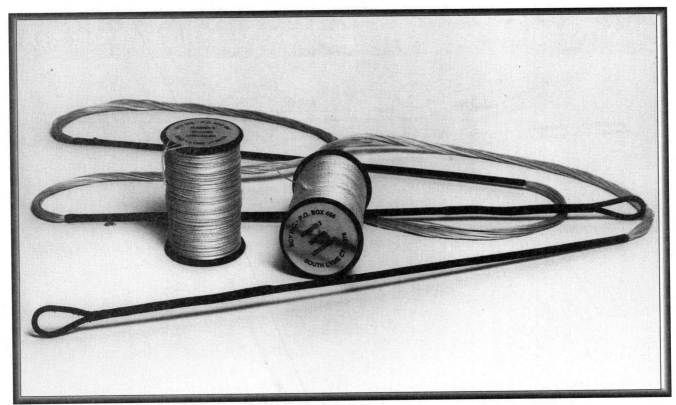

STREAM LINE - a new super fiber used in making bowstrings. Courtesy BCI Inc.

apply a touch of the lacquer thinner. This will remove both strand color and wax. Rub the loose strands dry with a paper towel. Now pull the ends together and apply about one inch of clear or white fiber on each piece of the loose strands. Pull these two cleaned sections together and make a black mark with a Sharpie pen. These two small black marks will provide a centering point, enabling you to tie off the loose strand ends, leaving a knotted loop equal in length to the other endless loops.

Loosen one string post bracket to give a small amount of slack, then slide the bundle of loop strands around the posts several times. This action helps to equalize the length of each loop. Now place the rest of the string back under tension again, placing a piece of waxed paper between the loopknot and the other strands.

Step 7:

This step could be hazardous to your health. It describes how to apply a form of "superglue" to the loopknot. Read the instructions on how to use this type of glue, and have a small open container of lacquer thinner open and available before doing so. It sets up extremely fast. You can easily end up gluing your fingers together — or almost anything your glue-moistened fingers touch within a few seconds. Keep these adhesives away from children.

To finish this knot, trim the strand ends about 1/2-inch from the knot. With a straightened paper clip, apply a tiny amount of Lok-Knot to the knot only. From then on, you can count on this loopknot staying put. Position the knot under the center serving approximately two inches from the bottom of the serving. When using an unwaxed string material, apply the

Felt Tip Pen Mark

Felt Tip Pen Mark

A **Fisherman's Knot** is used to complete the open loop of a continuous loop bowstring. Hold the loose ends of the string material side by side and clean about one inch of each strand with lacquer thinner. Make a mark across the loose strands with a felt tip pen. Complete the loop as shown and just before you pull the knot tight apply one minute drop of Stren Lok-Knot. Read the caution warning on the Lok-Knot package.

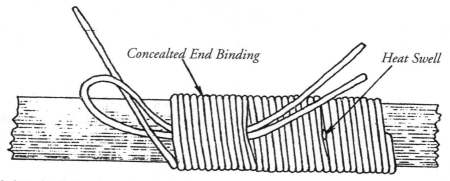

Concealted End Binding

Heat Swell

A **Concealed End Binding** is used to make bowstring end loops and the bowstring center serving. It also anchors nocking points, kisser buttons, and bowstring peep sights. Carefully heat swell each end of the strand material to complete the binding.

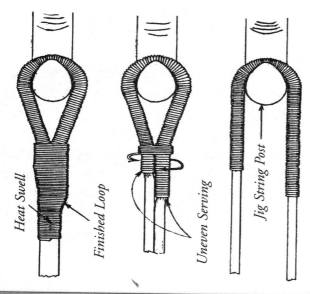

Heat Swell

Finished Loop

Uneven Serving

Jig String Post

One end of the loop forming material should be about twelve inches long and the other should be long enough to completely serve the loop and bowstring below recurve contact when the bow is at rest. Double wrap the end loop with the long and short lengths of serving to pull the loop together. After 6-8 double loops lay the short end down the string and wrap it into the loop with the longer serving. Complete the serving by using a concealed end binding and heat swell the long strand.

proper kind of wax to the string and burnish it in with a small piece of leather. If waxed material is being used, wax the loopknot area and burnish the string.

Step No. 8:

Tie a short piece of string to mark the center of one end of the bowstring and turn the string post bracket across the jig. With the short string as a center mark, serve a length sufficient to cover the string loops, tear drops or string posts. Allowing the served loop ends to exceed each other about 1/4 inch will help make a smoother finished serving. Check the location of the loopknot and finish the other string loop. Turn both stringpost brackets in line with the jig, placing the bracket posts holding the string to the inside of the jig.

Step No. 9:

Serve a short length of the bowstring with the monofilament center serving material. Check this served portion for proper arrownock string groove fit. If the fit is too tight, decrease the size of the monofilament; if it is too loose, increase the monofilament size (using monofilament test strength is a good way to judge monofilament diameter size). When buying monofilament, look for mill ends that are available as fishing leaders. I use Maxima for servings because several different sizes are available on my fishing reels.

A poor string groove fit on a factory string can be replaced by changing monofilament size. Nock an arrow and point the bow and arrow towards the floor. If the arrow falls free it is too loose, but if the arrow remains on the string, apply a light blow to the string, forcing the arrow to fall free. If the arrow doesn't fall, the serving is too tight. You should reduce the serving

diameter. If the string groove is too tight, you'll have problems with bow tuning and a loss in velocity. If the fit is too loose, the arrow will fall off the bowstring when the bow is drawn.

Now that we have determined serving size, estimate the nock point location by comparing the new serving location to an old string. Start the new center serving about 1 to 1 1/4 inches above the estimated nocking point. Extend the new serving down the string about two inches below the loopknot The center serving should finish out 7 to 9 inches long.

Step No. 10:

Insert the new string and measure the fistmele several times over a short period of time to determine at what point the string stops increasing in length. Temporarily locate the nocking point, kisser button and string peep until the string is "shot in," usually after about 100 shots.

Some archers consider the tension exerted by a compound's limbs enough to settle a string. If you prefer this lazy method, give it a couple of days. I feel that any new string needs to be properly "shot-in." But you can make your own "shot-in" measurements and finalize your string accessories.

After "shooting-in" the string, you may proceed with making another string. Remove the first handmade string with accessories intact and install the second handmade string. Wrap the first string — now fully complete and ready to shoot — around a piece of stiff cardboard. Then wrap it in aluminum foil. You are now prepared should disaster overtake the second string.

Refer to the page on knots and finishing for tips on tying the knots and whip finishes used in bowstring making. Follow the instructions and pay attention to the cautionary advice when using the fast-setting super-glue adhesives. ▲

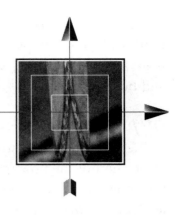

CHAPTER TWENTY-SIX

The Flemish Twist String

or centuries, the Flemish Twist was the ultimate in bowstrings wherever hemp fiber was available. The 1920s and '30s may have marked a big improvement in the recurve bow, but the hemp string stayed with us until after World War II. The braiding and twisting of all kinds of fibers was a common hobby once the 20th century arrived, with archers possessing the knowledge to turn the common hemp fiber into a dandy bowstring. A Flemish string can be a creeping disaster with the new bowstring materials and slick synthetic waxes, so use either Brownell's unwaxed B-S0 or BCY's B-500 for your string material. You'll also need a cake of pure beeswax instead of synthetic wax to complete the task properly.

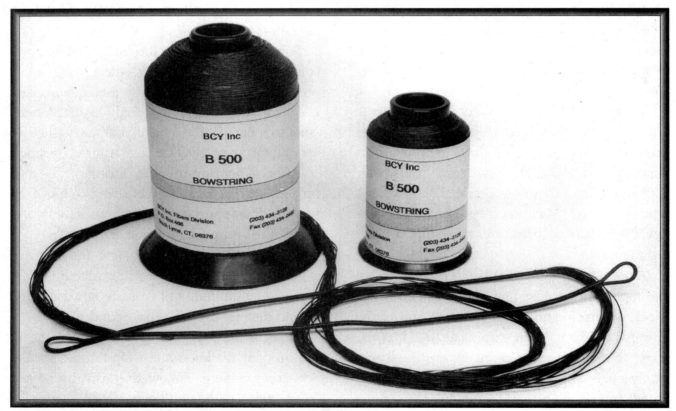

B 500 bowstring material. This is suitable for a modern "Flemish Twist" bowstring. Courtesy BCI Inc.

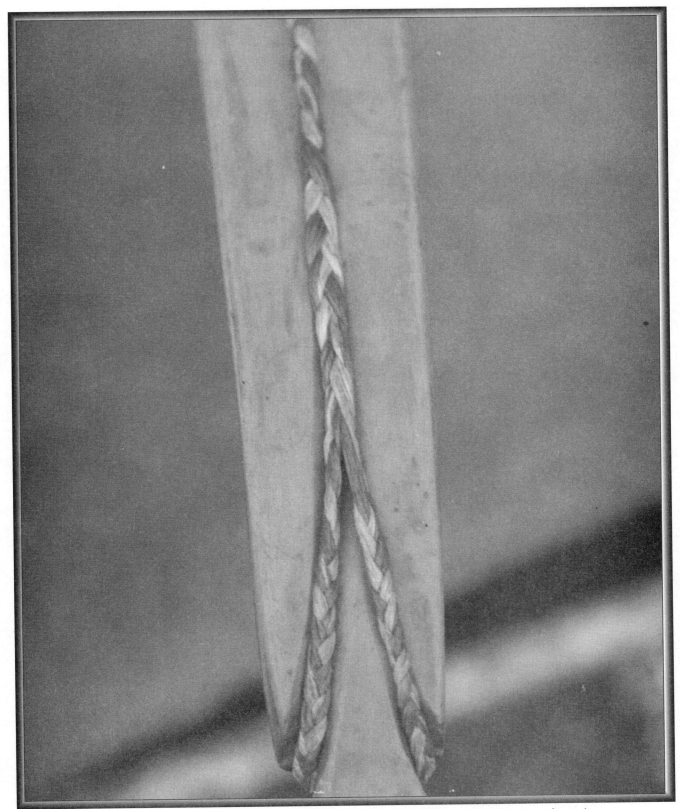

A bow tip showing the unusual pattern obtained when you braid or twist material of two or more colors into a bowstring.

Step 1:

Measure your strung bowstring from the start of the stationary loop on the bottom limb and the start of the sliding loop on the upper limb, then add two inches. Multiply this length by the number of strands desired.

Step 2:

Add another 48 inches to make the stationary and sliding loops. You now have the total length of material for the string.

Step 3:

Cut the number of strands required. I suggest a string in multiples of three (12-15-18 strands), simply because I like to use a three-plat to braid the loop ends back into the bowstring.

Step 4:

Make the stationary loop about 18 twists, bringing the remaining 20 to 21 inches of string back over the bowstring. Secure the loop to the edge of a table, covering the twisted loop with a small piece of leather and clamp with a small "C" clamp.

Start a braid into the string and continue for about 8 inches down the bowstring. Begin cutting one strand end off every 2 or 3 braids, making a tapered finish as it is braided into the bowstring. Secure this finish in place with masking tape and make the sliding loop using 22 to 24 twists.

Step 5:

At this point, start applying slight pressure and you'll see some real magic unfold. Remove

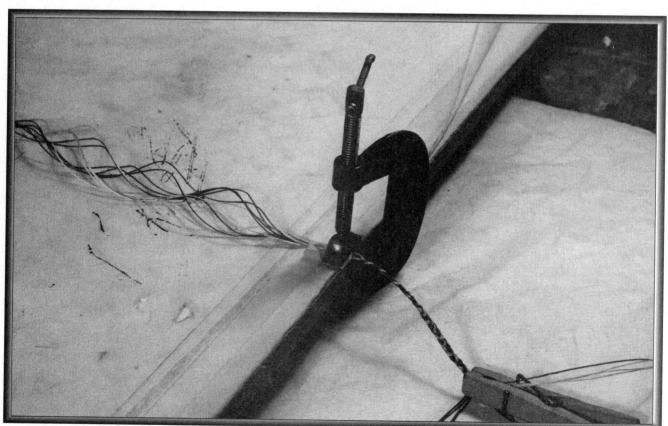

#1: Braiding for a stationary loop. Note how handy a clothes pin can be.

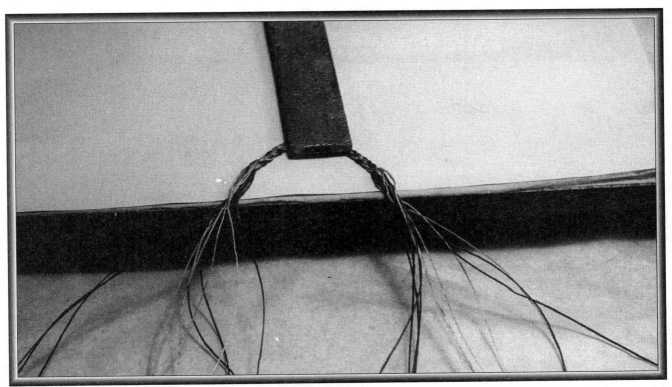

#2: Forming the stationary loop and matching the strands to braid the bowstring.

#3: The loop is formed and clamped. The first five inches of the bowstring is braided and you are ready to start cutting off the short strands.

MAKING A "FLEMISH TWIST" BOWSTRING

Basic 3-Braid Pattern Used In Making Many Of The Modern Flemish Bowstrings.

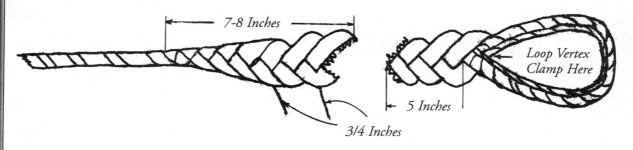

7-8 Inches

Loop Vertex
Clamp Here

5 Inches

3/4 Inches

The name "Flemish Twist" is a very popular misnomer. The act of twisting has turned into a braid. The hemp material has been replaced with dacron. There is a good reason, braiding holds dacron much better than twisting. To make a modern version of this string use unwaxed B-50 dacron and beeswax.

A. String your bow and measure to the vertex of each loop then add 3/4" to that length. Add another 60" for loop forming. This 60" allows plenty of length to form your loops and then braid back into the bowstring. Multiply the overall length by the number of strands needed for your bowstring.

B. Start at the vertex of your stationary loop and clamp the strands to a table edge using a small "C" clamp and a piece of leather. Start braiding the 30" length and duplicate the circumference of the old bowstring loop. Bend the braided portion into a loop. Check the size of the loop and clamp the strands at the loop vertex to the edge of the table. If you use black and white string material place the white strands together. Divide the black into two groups of black and one of white to make your braid. About every inch hold the braided strands and separate the remainder of the 30" strands. If you used unwaxed dacron they separate fairly easy. If you used waxed material they tend to stick together. Complete five inches of braiding and cut one of the short strands off leaving about 3/4" sticking out to be trimmed off later. Cut off one strand about every fifteen braids and you will have a braided taper reducing in size to the desired number of strands. Make sure that the strand that you cut off is one of the short lengths. When you cut off your last short strand hold the braided taper in place with a piece of masking tape until the other half of the string is braided and the string is given it's first waxing.

C. Reverse the string and duplicate step B. Make allowance for a larger sliding loop. Measure your distance between the loop vertexes now and remember the 3/4" length to twist the string after your braiding is complete.

D. Place your stationary loop on the bottom bowtip and start twisting the string. When you feel that the overall length is about right string the bow. If the fistmele is O.K. cut the short 3/4" strings off your braided taper and wax the string very thoroughly. Get this string warm with your burmish leather. Now make your center serving. This string will take 100-125 shots to settle-in and be ready for your fine tuning.

the sliding loop from the "C" clamp and place the stationary loop over the clamp spindle. Start twisting the string in a clockwise direction. When the string is short enough, place the sliding loop over the upper limb after working some beeswax into both loops.

Place the stationary loop on the lower limb and string the bow. Apply pure beeswax to the remainder of the bowstring and burnish the wax into the string with a piece of leather.

Make your center serving, locate the nocking point, and shoot the string in. You may have to shorten the string by further twisting, but limit this twisting to no more than 70 turns. If you need more, shorten the strand length between loops on future strings.

Having covered the basic steps of the Flemish Twist, some additional tips on mastering the Flemish Twist follow. First, Dacron B50 and B500 work reasonably well with pure beeswax, but the more modern synthetic waxes can mean a slow but steady increase in string length. This increase occurs because the Flemish Twist fails to hold the newer modern fibers. When treated with the newer synthetic waxes, you may have a disaster on your hands.

Several companies advertise custom Flemish strings, with jigs and instructions — and even videos — available. I'm not sure they can produce non-stretching Flemish Strings with the superfibers and synthetic waxes. Tradition is fine, but a new recurve is built for today's materials with a properly constructed superfiber continuous loop string, can out perform any other bowstring. ▲

Ollie Morgan measuring fistmele by using his fist and thumb. This is the time honored way of checking bowstring let-down while in competition. Ollie's grin displays his pleasure with his new longbow.

CHAPTER TWENTY-SEVEN

Important Bowhunting Accessories

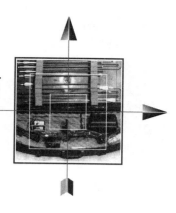

 What is the most valuable accessory for a bowhunter? A practical answer is the accessory container that you carry into the woods. Whatever you leave at home won't be worth much should the need arise. That's why the container just may be the most important bowhunting accessory.

A large number of personal packing containers are available to modern bowhunters. The popular "Fanny Pack" is simply too small for anything but a one-day hunt in familiar territory. If you plan on a short hunt in unfamiliar territory, carry a larger pack containing some overnight survival equipment. (see the chapter on "Roaming The Woods"). My

Guy Hickman displays his Arkansas Tusk Hog to Phil Smith. A trophy like this is not a common event and happens only when the successful hunter selects the proper equipment and accessories. **Courtesy Phil Smith**

Bill Hogue with an Arkansas Bottomland Rattlesnake. Note his wearing of "snake chaps".

choice for a backpack is the World War II musette bag. It requires traveling to a military surplus store to find one, but while you're there you can also pick up a "Pistol Belt" and a low-priced canteen. The contents of your pack should rate survival first, then the accessories that will help you succeed with your hunting. Listed below are a number of accessories one might choose to include in an accessory bag.

✦ *The small brass "nock rings" used to set up your bow have almost become standard equipment. Installing these nock rings is best done with a pair of crimping pliers equipped with a nock ring-opening device. This certainly qualifies as a very handy accessory to include in your container bag. Try the Pro Model Crimping Tool produced by the Tru Fire Corporation.*

✦ *Other accessories to pack are the nock height locating devices known as "bow squares". The*

A rubber bow tip protector is used to protect the lower bow tip from ground contact. Protector by Bear Archery Co.

Using a short hunting stabilizer.

Potawatome Square best serves aluminum and wood arrows. BPE's tool screws into a carbon arrow outsert (or an aluminum arrow insert) and is accurate while setting up a shoot-through arrowrest.

◆ *Stabilizers were first designed to help control torque or twisting of the bow as it was shot. Later an inverted "V" stabilizer helped to keep a bow in a vertical position when shooting International rules for Olympic-type competition using recurve bows. The arrival of the extremely short compound bows has inspired the design of stabilizers that act more like shock absorbers. Browning Archery produces some extremely short stabilizers that are loaded with mercury, which brings back memories of the Ben Pearson Sovereign Bows featuring a mercury-loaded stabilizer and two mercury-loaded capsules built into the handle riser to absorb shock.*

One of my secrets to success. We have used this scent cover for twelve years. Spray your boots, crotch, and armpits. It will cover human scent real well.

Two small compact flashlights. Shown are the Mini-Maglite and the Duracell.

Some stabilizers are loaded with springs to absorb shock. Hunting stabilizers are usually about 12 inches in length; target stabilizers can be considerably longer. Stabilizer shafts can be telescopic and constructed of many materials, including aluminum or carbon. If used, you'll notice a difference in the way a stabilizer-equipped bow feels as it is shot. I like a 12-inch solid shaft stabilizer for hunting and a 32-inch Easton stabilizer for 3 D.

♦ *To prevent "heeling" or "torquing" a bow while shooting, some archers use a wrist strap to prevent the bow from jumping out of their hand. These straps are so popular that most archery shops keep them in stock. They ease your mind, and let you concentrate on aim and release. They are also an excellent preventive accessory that eliminates "grabbing" the bow as it is shot.*

The smoothest finger release occurs when using a good tab and the bowstring is filling the first groove in your fingers. The Wilson Tab has filled this job for many years.

Golden Eagle Ind. markets a powerful small flashlight combined with a distress strobe. Courtesy Golden Ind. and Seitz Adv.

♦ The Game Tracker Co. makes what it calls the "Spare Finger," a device that holds an arrow in place on an arrowrest and releases it at the start of the draw. The bow can hang from a limb or a hook, and when you need it the arrow will be securely in place. This eliminates the need for placing the arrow on the bow while game is close by.

♦ Three basic types of arrow quivers are available to choose from when selecting this necessary accessory. The oldest is the back or shoulder quiver, the traditional method for transporting arrows ever since Noah unloaded the ark. This type of quiver was also noted for bending or warping wood-shafted arrows (it was never meant to store arrows). The required practice on the village green probably fathered the belt quiver, while modern times produced the bow quiver. All three are suitable for hunting or target.

The 'Trimlite' 400 Cordura Belt Quiver by Neet. Primarily a 3-D or target quiver the Camo indicated light bowhunting use. Courtesy Hawk Assoc. and Neet Products Inc.

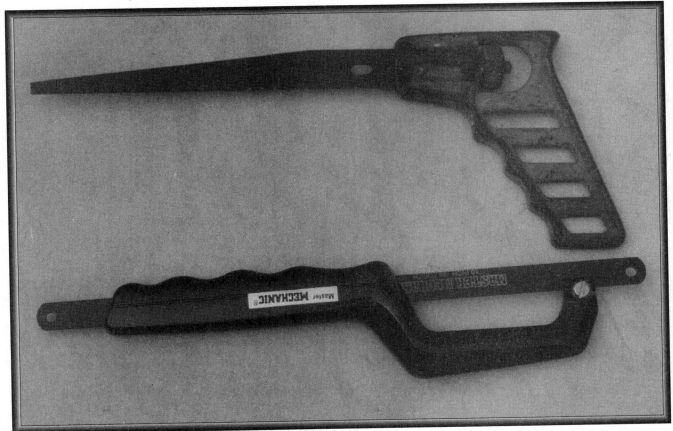

Two small saws. They are small, easy to transport and they cut bone and wood.

When hunting, make sure the bow quiver can be removed and attached to the stand or other convenient place. Removing a quiver as you take your stand and start hunting can prevent spooking game. The sudden movement of a bright or white fletched arrow can cause game to flinch or duck an arrow. Being old fashioned, I like a shoulder quiver, while two of my sons use belt quivers designed for hunting.

◆ *The arm guard is another piece of equipment often overlooked or not used since the arrival of the compound bow. It's a necessity when shooting the long bow or recurve. With the more open shooting stance used with the compound, the arm guard can be discarded (which explains why some compound users do not even own one).*

Wearing an arm guard in winter and cold weather also serves to hold your jacket sleeve out of the path of the bowstring. Wearing a long arm guard in cold weather is just good insurance when a shot presents itself.

◆ *The shooting glove has been a major means of finger protection and still finds favor with traditional long bow and recurve shooters. The heavy draw weight of these bows oftentimes caused grooves to form just over the finger joints, producing poor releases. Modern times have seen the shooting tab replace the glove with many archers. The Wilson Tab is the standard by which all other shooting tabs are measured, having won honors and gold medals in international competition over the years. I have used the Wilson Tab since the mid '50s, taking game under all types of conditions (except rain). It has never let me down.*

◆ *When bowhunting from a tree, the Loggy Bayou Climbing Stand will serve you quite well. For strength, weight, climbing ability, comfort*

Shooting the PSE Inferno with a Bomar Stabilizer

A "hard case" is good protection while transporting your equipment. It also prevents leaving needed equipment at home.

Another Arkansas Bottomland Rattlesnake. Just one more reason to use a small flashlight at night.

and security, this stand is a first-class accessory for bowhunters.

I have three Purdy Widow Makers that are at least 17 years old and still in mint condition. Several of our ladder stands are home-built of wood. They are well protected from moisture by frequent painting and the use of roofing plastic. These wooden stands, however, are often weakened by squirrels who like to chew on the plywood seats. Always inspect a stand several times during the hunting season, whether it is made of metal or wood. Tree stand breakage is a major cause of hunter injury.

✦ Safety belts offer excellent protection, but they can cause problems too. A safety belt should be strong enough to support a sudden fall or the collapse of a stand collapse. Fortunately, most falls tend to pull you into the tree as the stand

Get a handful of bowstring with that Tab-just as if you are picking up a bucket full of water. Put that bowstring firmly in the first grooves of your fingers. Drawing a bow with the string across your finger tips can cause tendinitis in your forearm. The famed Wilson Tab is shown here well trimmed to the archer's fingers.

An item for your pack. This Finger Ring Cable Saw is light and inexpensive plus it works.

collapses. Since weight exerts a pressure on a safety belt, you may have problems as the belt tightens about your body. Make sure the belt will enable you to free yourself in an emergency situation. Hold onto the tree trunk with your legs and one arm, then free yourself with the other. The odds will turn in your favor as you "coon" or slide down the tree to safety.

To install a safety belt properly, attach the belt around the tree trunk with snug — but not tight — tension. There should be enough slack between the tree trunk belt and your body belt so that you can stand or sit comfortably.

✦ *Game scents can make the difference between success or failure in hunting, so make them an additional accessory to pack away in your bag. Scents cause game to react one way, then react differently the next time the scent is encountered.*

Use an arm guard to compress your coat sleeve during cold weather bowhunts.

An archer using a wrist strap.

A subordinate buck will often leave an area where a few drops of "Doe in Estrus" have been "planted," because he senses the dominant buck will show up and administer a first class horning. Scents may even cause the dominant buck to leave an area when he senses the scent is much stronger than it should be. He knows instinctively that no doe in his territory is about to come in season.

It's always advisable to use an estrus scent sparingly. Apply no more than two or three drops to a cotton ball tied to a short length of dark fishing line. Carry this ball sealed tightly in a wide mouth jar. Drape the ball and string across a low limb where it will position your trophy animal properly Remember to remove the scented ball and string whenever you leave the stand. Never place any game scent on your clothing or boots. "Doe in Estrus" scents can cause strange behavior from many domestic animals and can lead to

personal attack. Bulls and stallions especially become very aggressive when encountering this odor. Cover scents such as fox urine or skunk scent may or may not work; I have very little faith in using them. And skunk scent can cause serious nausea in a very short time.

Another type of scent that doesn't imitate an animal odor is called Arm and Hammer Deodorizing Air Freshener. This "baking soda in a can" has been altered with several different odors, all of which seem to disguise human odor effectively. The odor of preference, however, is the "Pet Fresh" odor in this series. We first used this deodorizer in the early '80s and it has been a top-notch success. My most impressive trial occurred when an adult doe and her fawn walked down a trail just ten minutes after I had passed down that trail without being detected. I've had lots of confidence in this deodorizer

A well concealed bowhunter

Using a fleeced lined hip quiver - a pouch for bowhunting.

ever since. Whenever I go hunting, I spray this air freshener inside and outside my pants and shirt then across the soles of my boots.

✦ All serious bowhunters should set a goal of owning a good hard case to protect their equipment while it's being transported. Arriving at a hunting site and finding your bow damaged will get the message across in a dramatic fashion. The case can also be used to store arrows between hunts.

✦ "Forward of Center" formula is a measurement that tells why one set of arrows is more stable than another. Saunders Archery produces an expanding tape that helps determine your F. O. C. balance percentage.

✦ A good magnetic compass to add to your pack can be found in any sporting goods department. Most are inexpensive and reasonable in quality. Silva and Brunton offer a wide range of compass models to select from.

✦ Walking to a stand a full hour before daylight is a common practice that requires one to carry a small flashlight. Take care not to shine these lights up into the trees, because you'll alarm game at a considerable distance from your path. Keep these lights shining on the ground as you walk. One predawn encounter with a canebrake rattlesnake or cottonmouth moccasin laying in your path will make you a believer in the use of a flashlight.

✦ Game Tracker Inc. markets a simple bowhunting device called "The Game Tracker." It's an archery version of the fisherman's spinning reel. This tracking device should be mounted on your bow in close proximity to the arrow. A hit on a trophy animal will cause a white or orange monofilament line to adhere to that animal and act as an aid in its recovery. This game-finding unit is almost mandatory when embarking on a guided bear hunt. Many game animals are taken within 30 yards, so a shot at this distance can bring down many other animals besides black bears. Lack of monofilament motion can tell you much about the condition of a wounded animal. ▲

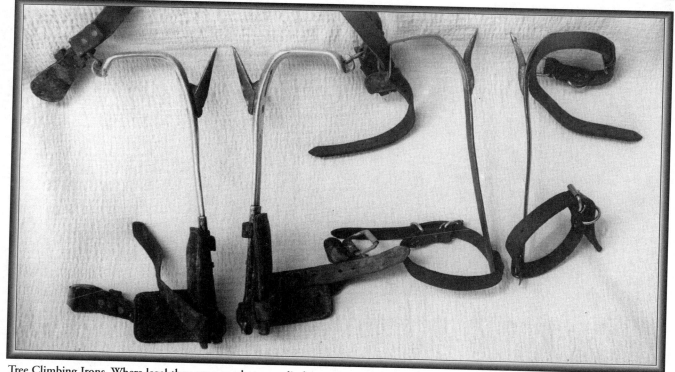

Tree Climbing Irons. Where legal they are a good way to climb a tree.

CHAPTER TWENTY-EIGHT

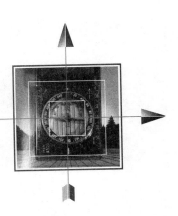

How To Use The Magnetic Compass

agnetism was known in ancient times wherever iron was worked. The Chinese are generally credited with inventing the magnetic compass, which led to the discovery of the magnet's relationship to the North Star. A magnetic compass will indicate "magnetic north" while the North Star shows the "true north." For early man, the difference between the true pole and the magnetic pole was often close enough to allow him to travel to a distant goal and return home safely. The difference between true north and magnetic north was probably discovered by early seafaring captains.

The early Spanish and Portuguese sailors were the real leaders in sea navigation. They had an uncanny ability to craft a workable compass. They also had available a material they called "cork." This may seem trivial, but cork proved the best way to float a slender piece of magnetized steel in a bowl of water mounted where the helmsman could see it. Those seafaring people from the Spanish peninsula can lay claim to transforming the magnetic compass into a practical tool for locating direction.

Only a few years behind the Spaniards in the development of ocean-traveling ships and navigation technology were the English. Our "longitude" and "latitude" lines are examples of work in this field. These seafaring nations gave us long-range navigation skills, but the small pocket compass had to wait for the technology to catch up. Modern construction techniques have made the portable pocket compass accurate to about 300 feet in a mile, ensuring accuracy for the walking bowhunte. Its inexpensive cost also makes the compass a might handy piece of bowhunting equipment.

Three basic forms of the magnetic compass are considered suitable for today's outdoorsman. All three depend on a directional indicator to point toward magnetic north. The accuracy of these compasses also depends on how well the indicating needle can be aligned with the compass dial, hence establishing the course one must follow.

Magnetic north has recently been discovered to be a mass of molten iron — located east of true north — that is constantly moving. Your position, this magnetic iron mass, and true north all form what is known as the "Angle of Declination". It depends on your location and whether you are located on one of the coasts or in mid-America. This "Angle of Declination" is printed on geodetic survey maps, but its location changes with time (for a current figure or recently updated map, contact the Corps of Engineers). When planning a one- to three-day hike that runs north and south, don't even consider this angle. Watch the number of check points, if

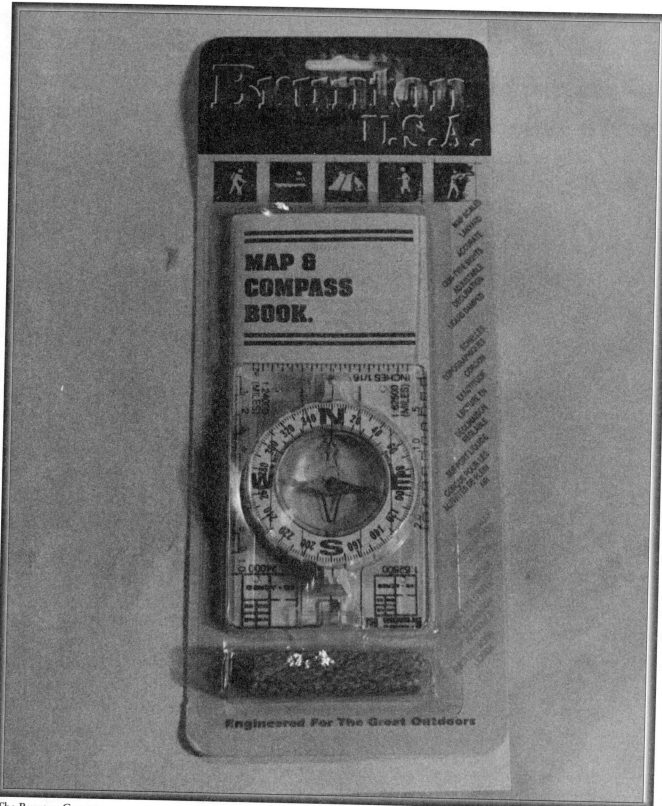

The Brunton Compass

The Silva Compass

available. It would be rare indeed for declination to pose a problem on a foot journey. There's no way to shield a pocket compass from the magnetic attraction of metallic objects that are close by or attached to your body. Any effective shield will block out some degree of attraction from the magnetic pole and reduce accuracy.

The most common compass is a simple magnetized needle mounted on a vertical axis, enabling it to move over a fixed circular chart marked in directions and degrees. This chart and needle indicator are mounted in a container resembling a pocket watch case. These models are sometimes equipped with simple sighting equipment. The circular case is what gives this compass its moniker: "watch compass".

The *lensatic* compass is slightly larger and usually has a better built case, providing greater distance between the markings on the dial. The lens is often magnifying and the sighting equipment is sturdier and more refined in its construction. The design of this compass generally favors more open country. Its cost can range from moderate to expensive depending on size, case design and construction.

The *prismatic* compass features a directional indicator that floats in liquid. A popular model looks as if someone had placed directional marks and degrees on a small round ball and floated it in a container filled with liquid. Another type is flat, with a circular dial floating in a watch case. When travelling in a territory where you know the basic return direction, having a compass is good insurance should the sun be obscured. When heading into unfamiliar territory, always lay a course that will get you back to the starting point. As a case in point, my longtime friend and hunting companion, Dr. James L. Smith, was elk hunting in the mountains around Monte Vista, Colorado one day, when the sun became blocked out at one point. He checked his compass and started back, but after a short time sensed that he should have seen familiar surroundings — possibly even Monte Vista. Certain that something was not right with his compass, he followed his instinct and reversed direction for a short time. Soon it was dark enough for him to see the lights of Monte Vista — and safety. I don't recommend following your instincts over compass directions, but this man happens to be a skilled woodsman and, in this instance, it paid off.

After Dr. Smith's safe return, it was determined that his compass had been carried in close proximity to his steel-cased flashlight. Doubtless, the flashlight had reversed the polarity of his compass.

To gain confidence in your compass and your ability to use it, pay close attention to the exercises that follow:

◆ *Begin by acquainting yourself with the various parts of your compass. Most inexpensive watch compass dials are marked every five degrees, with major directional marks at North (0°), East (90°), South (180°) and West (270°). Degrees continue in a clockwise direction with the circle compled at the North marker. Make note of the minor points at Northeast, Southeast, Southwest, and Northwest. Note too that one hour of wrist watch time consumes 30 degrees compass direction.*

Learn to hold the compass flat and level while moving it slowly in a half circle. This is a check for anything magnetic that may be on your person or in close proximity. It only takes a few seconds and could prevent a serious mistake in navigation. When up and about at daybreak, look at the sun as it starts to climb into the horizon. Align the north mark on the compass dial with the north indicating needle and align your wrist watch dial with 12 o' clock pointing north. Next, take a

The Brunton and Silva Compass

sighting on the rising sun – your compass reading should indicate 90° and your watch about 3 o' clock (depending on daylight saving or standard time). Remember, the sun will be south of the equator during our winter months; and when North America's summer occurs the sun lies north of the equator. Coordinating the location of the sun, wrist watch time and compass is not difficult. Get in the habit of glancing at them whenever you use the compass.

◆ *Another sighting exercise involves finding yourself in a square city block. Start at the northeast corner of the block and sight down the street to the southeast corner. After walking down to that corner, sight 90° to the southwest corner. From there, sight 90° to the northwest corner and proceed to that corner. Notice that you have now walked parallel to your first block — but in the reverse direction. Note also that you have not counted steps or measured distance; but upon returning to the southeast corner you will be close enough to step on it. This exercise is a basic method for teaching us how to sight across a simple compass, not to mention the importance of traveling a reasonably straight line.*

◆ *The next exercise involves taking a bearing after travelling south down a north-south street. Call this "First Street." Go south until you cross two streets running east and west, then turn east until you have crossed two streets running north and south. Call this street "Third Street". Now, take another north-south reading. It should look the same as the reading you took back on First Street. Should you proceed on this same sighting down Third Street, you'll miss the intended destination at the end of First Street by two city blocks. In theory, you've formed a triangle with one point on First Street, the second point on Third Street, and the magnetic pole serving as the third point. A pocket compass is simply not capable of reflecting these minute differences.*

To understand the importance of the foregoing exercise, let's go to a deer camp and follow this hypothetical trip. A hunting buddy leaves you instructions to "take a compass course of 170° from camp and walk for twenty minutes. You should intersect a white oak ridge loaded with acorns and be in sight of that ladder stand that I put up last Friday." You start out on the course and after ten minutes you are distracted by a deer running off. You follow the deer to see what it was feeding on. You then resume your compass course for the remaining ten minutes only to discover that you've missed the white oak ridge and can't find the ladder stand. You missed it by the distance you wandered away from the original course ten minutes away.

Should you find it necessary to leave your original course, please mark the spot with blaze orange ribbon so that you can return to that same spot and resume the original course. By so doing, you'll have a much better chance of finding your hunting buddy's ridge and his stand.

Carrying a map in your pack makes good sense when hunting or hiking. Geodetic survey maps are fine, but a large scale map of your territory should be available from your local or state County Agriculture or Highway departments. An aeronautical chart obtained from a local flying service also indicates true north and the angles of declination lines pointing out magnetic north. These charts are used by private pilots to compute their true headings, wind drift, ground speed and other performance factors.

Instead of buying one expensive model, onsider purchasing several inexpensive compasses. That way you can keep a compass in your quiver, fanny pack, and glove compartment. Remember, the compass you forgot to bring along won't help much on your next hunt.   ▲

CHAPTER TWENTY-NINE

How To Use The GPS

Show me a woods-roaming hunter who has never been lost and I'll show you a hunter who has always hunted close to the road or rarely ventured out of sight of his pickup. Hunt with men like Lewis Rush, Bill Clements or Bill Hogue and you'll be amazed at how they can hunt in strange woods or follow coon hounds all night, then return to their trucks with no apparent effort. On one memorable occasion, Rush and I followed a light blood trail as the sun was setting. Suddenly the deer crossed the fence line of a densely wooded area. We knew that if we quit the trail now it would be blown over with leaves or faded out by morning. So, we set our bows and quivers outside the fence line and kept after that deer.

Learning to use and build confidence in using a GPS around a local airport.

The Magellan GPS 2000. Courtesy Magellan Systems Corp.

There was no moon, no visible stars, and a lot of very black night. We found the deer and put it on a pole, and neither of us said anything. Somehow that deer-loaded pole and the fence line came together at the spot where our bows and quivers were leaning against a large white oak tree. And on two different treks with Bill Hogue, a short walk luckily placed us on an old trail, enabling us to make it back to the truck both times. I have mentioned these incidents to show that getting "slightly confused' can happen to anyone.

Many times I have wondered how Daniel Boone and others of his day roamed the dense forests of America. Their time schedules were flexible and they had no friendly neighbors along the way to help guide them on their explorations. These men knew how to walk the woods, but even they admitted to becoming "confused."

The first time I heard the letters "GPS" was during "Desert Storm." We began to hear stories then about a hand-held device that could extract magic from satellites placed in the sky and help

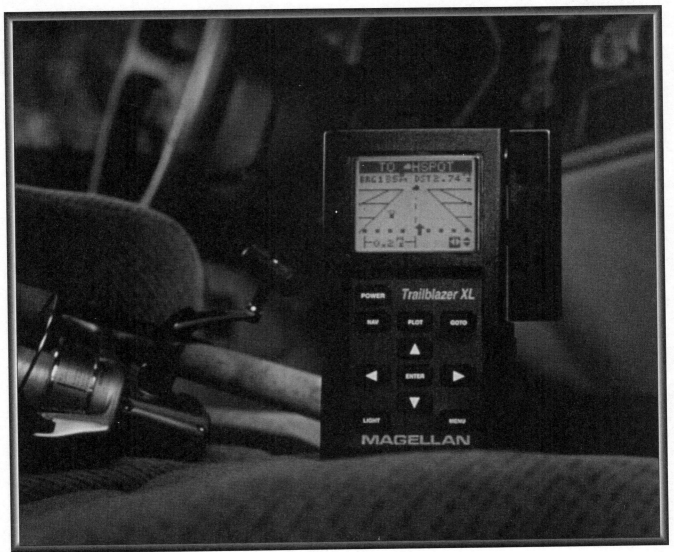

Trailblazer XL

GPS 4000

GPS 2000

The Trailblazer XL, GPS 4000 and GPS 2000

guide lost souls to their destination. The first users of the "Geographical Positioning System" were the military, but this technology is now showing up everywhere. The Magellan GPS 2000 Satellite Navigator is more than impressive in its performance. This small, 10-ounce shirt-pocket gadget can steer you anywhere on earth. It's not meant for extreme long range navigation, but with a little ingenuity on your part it can go wherever you want to go. That big 18-wheeler that just passed you on the Interstate is equipped with — or soon will be — the GPS. His dispatcher knows where he is at any one time. Rumor has it that weigh station officers can plug into a truck's GPS and tell exactly what that truck has been doing for the past several hours.

This new system recently assisted authorities in Arkansas when a driver's dispatcher told the local Sheriff that a suspected driver was parked at a distant truck stop and was asleep. The Sheriff telephoned ahead, had the driver awakened, and placed in custody.

There are now 24 satellites in the U.S. circling the earth, all paid for by our tax dollars. These satellites and the small, inexpensive GPS units fit in well with the activities of outdoorsmen. The Magellan 2000, for example, fills the needs of a bowhunter very well. Not only will it help locate a certain location in your woods, it will take you to a stand, locate a dead deer, then point out the closest route back to camp.

Tekeze River Expedition

The first task when acquiring a GPS device is to be able to communicate with it. Read your owner's manual and identify what each button will do. If you can't tell this gadget what you want then it obviously can't take you where you want to go. Begin by "initializing" the device, i.e., telling the GPS where it is, how high it is, what time it is, and that you're ready to put it to work. Once that's done, turn to the chapter explaining how to clear the unit. This will build up your confidence should you feel responsible for "messing up." It's a simple matter to clear everything out and start over. I found out that my front yard was a very poor place to locate positions. Houses, overhead power lines, and GPSs are not too friendly toward each other, so get yourself into a clear area when using the system.

After reading the instructions again, I headed for the nearest airport, one with a road that almost encircled it. This place was made to order for getting acquainted and building up my confidence in using this new-found technology. My idea was to first establish a "landmark," then drive around the airport boundary and establish a "GoTo," which is the technical language for "how to go to" a location that already entered into the unit.

When I first used the system, I didn't give it time to "lock on" to the satellites that it needed to establish contact and tell me what I wanted to know. As soon as the "Navigation" screens indicated satellite contact I would punch the "GoTo" button and that's when the problems started. I discovered that there is a "Lock Icon" position indicator, and if I waited long enough for this "Lock On" to become visible I would begin to get along with this device. I could go around the airport and "establish a landmark," then drive around the boundary to another location and punch the "Go To" button. I would now be looking directly at the desired spot where the GPS indicated.

The Magellan 2000, which stores up to 100 landmarks, fills up in a hurry. I carry a maintenance log in my truck, so when I visit one of these areas I can get a "Position Fix" and record it and other pertinent data in my log book. When I return to this area I can re-enter those locations in my GPS. And in doing so, I can keep my GPS open and uncluttered for the camp trips that I love to take. Using my truck or campsite as a "landmark," I can then set up my deerstands and return to any of them without marking a trail. Using GPS also gives me a good feeling that some stranger will not be in my tree stand when I arrive, or that some other hunter will come wandering up to see where the marked trail leads.

The GPS Technology is rolling across this country faster than the supply can meet, so it may take only a short time to secure the unit of your choice. Put one on your "must have" list and feel confident that the short wait is worth it. This new technology can be fun and very helpful in many way. It can also increase your outdoor safety; so, as Magellan may have once said: "Go have fun — and don't get lost." ▲

CHAPTER THIRTY

How To Use The Electronic Compass

 or centuries, the relationship of the magnetic compass needle and the North Star became an orientation point for location. Seafaring helmsmen or their captain-navigators may have discovered that the more level a magnetic compass was maintained the more accurate the compass readings would be. Floating a sliver of magnetized steel in a bowl of water was probably the first effort at mechanical compass leveling. As technology was improved, the presence of a magnetic pole came under scrutiny. The discovery of the sextant strengthened the suspicion of a magnetic pole, but real proof was delayed until the arrival of the early polar explorers.

The dictionary describes a gimbal as two metal rings that house and maintain the direction sensor in a level manner. Early "gimballing" began with a piece of magnetized steel suspended by a piece of rawhide or sinew to a magnetized sliver of steel floated in a bowl of water. A crude form of electronic gimballing was then developed.

George Hsu, an electronic engineer who specializes in directional instruments, discovered improvements and patented a more practical form of the electronic gimbal. His discoveries and additional work in the field made the electronic compass available to the modern outdoorsman. The "Outback" (which costs about $100) is a small pocket-sized instrument used by amateur and professional outdoorsmen. It has digital readout and a return mode to help hunters return to their camp or vehicle. Other features of the Outback include a backlighting mode for use at night, and a sighting arrangement for taking bearings on distant objects. There's also a choice of modes for the magnetic pole or true north with this device, which can pinpoint a fishing "honey hole" by triangulation.

This compass will also indicate if there's a magnetic field nearby that could affect an accurate reading. Should an "interference mode" be highlighted by minor interference, you can recalibrate the instrument by rotating two complete 360° turns while holding the compass level. This new navigation instrument is being improved rapidly, but like the magnetic compass or the GPS, it should be used before entering the woods — and you should also carry a spare set of batteries that will last approximately 12 hours. Utilizing the compass backlighting, however, will increase electrical demand and reduce battery life. ▲

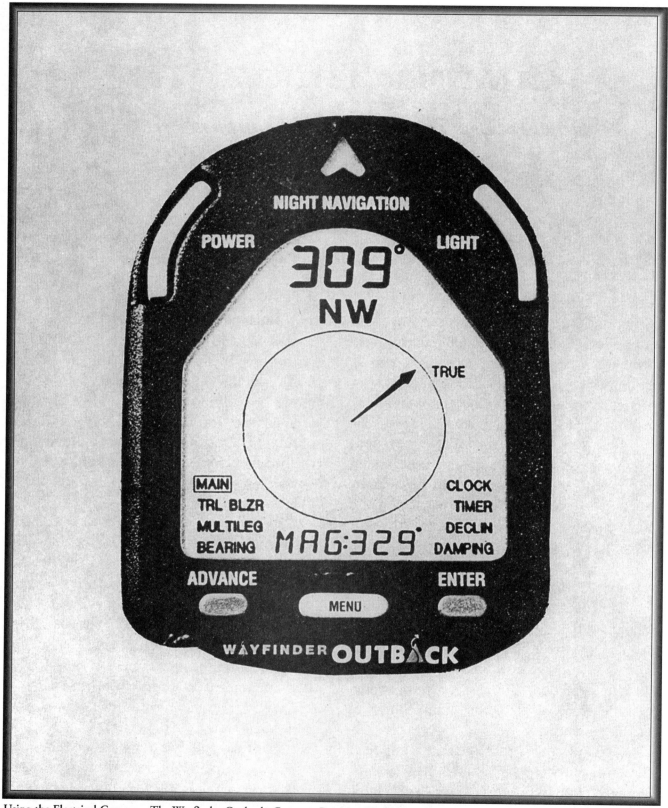

Using the Electrical Compass, The Wayfinder Outback. Courtesy Precision Navigation, Inc.

CHAPTER THIRTY-ONE

Spending Time In The Woods—Profitably

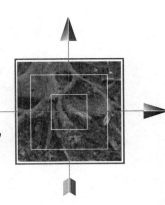

his may sound like a foolish question, but did you ever plan on getting lost while hunting? Don't kid yourself, it can happen, usually when you least expect it. Many people who pride themselves on their skill in the woods find it embarrassing even to consider the possibility of getting lost. Yet every year, we read articles in the local newspaper of hikers or hunters getting lost and spending one or more nights in the woods before being rescued.

People do strange and unpredictable things when they're lost. I still remember one story involving a Memphis doctor and his daughter who entered the woods about an hour before daylight one morning in Cotton Plant, Arkansas. Three days later, they were found by two squirrel hunters in what is now the Dagmar Wildlife Management Area, some 17 miles from their car. Their hunting clothes were shredded; their guns were lost. They had plastered themselves with mud for protection against mosquitoes.

These two people were so wild that they had to be caught and calmed down before they realized that they'd been found. A train had passed by a quarter of a mile away only ten minutes earlier, and they were within a mile of a major highway that connected Little Rock and Memphis. And yet the train and the highway traffic went unnoticed. Those lost souls were extremely stressed out, but happily they recovered after receiving medical help.

In another case, a squirrel hunter was lost for three days and nights in the White River Waterfowl Refuge. This strip of land was bordered on the north by a well-traveled entry road. The east boundary was the White River, and to the west was farmland with the fall harvest at its peak. The south boundary was another busy road that ran along on top of a levee. This strip of land was 16 miles long and three miles wide; there were the sounds of automobiles, boats, tractors, and crop combines; and yet they all went unnoticed. Obviously, this hunter never discussed with himself what he would do if he ever became lost. If he had just made himself comfortable and stayed put, someone would have found him.

About four years ago, a young hunter was placed on a deer stand by his grandfather, but he decided he could do better at another location. As night fell, the grandfather and several others started a major search. This young hunter, after walking by my son's Bronco, stopped in a heavy growth of broom sage grass and made himself a brush shelter. He spent the whole night there well sheltered while a search went on around him. He was within 50 yards of a gravel road and yet the search team passed close by several times during the night.

Bill Hogue examines a "deer tick."

So, now for the $64 questions: Just how do you go into the woods? Do you know your area well enough to be able to walk out at *anytime*? Are you *prepared* to spend the night? Just a few simple items can mean a comfortable night or a battle for survival. A 12-foot square of clear 6-mil plastic, a ball of 160- to 200-pound nylon string, one ten-inch candle, waterproof wood matches or two Zippo lighters, a simple cable saw, and a quart canteen of drinking water are all a lost hunter needs to survive in most cases. Drop in a couple of high energy bars and you could spend the night dry, out of the wind, and sleep without feeling starved. Total weight (excluding the canteen full of water) is less than three pounds. If your bag doesn't contain a map and compass, then you probably deserve a night

in the woods. Those two items should be standard equipment when hunting in any large or strange territory. You can obtain maps outside your area as well. To do so, contact the nearest Corps of Engineers office or any available Federal Building. With an up-to-date geodetic survey map of your favorite hunting territory, you'll also learn something about land elevations and features within the area for cataloging in your mind. For example, Mother Nature seems to locate food-producing trees and vegetation according to the moisture that promotes growth. I have heard many hunters lament a poor acorn crop when often a difference of 200 or 300 feet in elevation meant the difference in good pollination, ample moisture and a good food crop.

Another feature about tracts of land not shown on any map are the sounds that can be heard from that area. A roadway that traverses a given area will produce sounds of auto traffic; a river or lake will generate the sounds of boat traffic; and twice a day the sounds of cattle will indicate the location of a farm. A jet airliner rising or descending can indicate the direction of an airport. Your hunting area would have to be very large or remote not to produce a few sounds of its own. Your knowledge of an area will also teach you how to compare familiar and strange territories. Map reading can help your success as a hunter as well as preventing you from becoming lost in the wilderness.

A good map points out more than how to get into and out of an area. Skillful interpretation can also point out areas of game concentration. A deer will travel a ridgetop in South Carolina, Georgia or the Ozarks, and on the flatter plateaus of the Rocky Mountains. Different foods are found at different elevations. A game animal crossing a mountain will travel a long way to use a pass through the Rockies or a cut in the Smokies. Learn to use these map clues to fill your game tag as well as finding your way back to camp.

A quart-sized canteen of water serves valuable mental and physical needs while hunting, whether at sea level or in the elevations of the

Timbo Bass used a mountain bike to pull his tree stand.

Rocky Mountain high country. There you'll discover that a craving for water is a major factor. Whether hunting on foot, horseback or driving a motor vehicle, it seems that the higher you are the greater the desire for a drink of water.

Modern technology seems to be crowding out the old paraffin-coated wind match so favored by many old-time woodsmen and substituting the mechanical lighter. Should you decide to use one, be sure to carry two in your belt pack. Cold weather can prevent these lighters from working; so if the first one doesn't work, warm up the second lighter by placing it under your armpit for about five minutes. If your belt pack will accommodate one, take along a large diameter candle for greater heat output and longer burn time. Another survival item is a plain plastic sheet about 12 feet on each side and six thousandths of an inch thickness. Learn to fold this plastic so that all possible trapped air is removed. A good folding pattern will reduce the size of the folded plastic and ensure easy storage. This plastic sheeting makes an excellent wind and rain shelter, and under cold and windy conditions it could easily be a life-saver.

The nylon cord included in your "survival pack" has unlimited uses, especially when used in combination with the plastic sheeting; simply lay the plastic over a small round object, pulling the plastic down and around it. Place a slip knot over the plastic-covered object and pull it tight. Do this at each corner of the plastic to make a weather shelter. By supporting the plastic in the center you can easily construct an "A" type shelter. Lay the plastic flat and fold it back over itself for protection from wind, rain and wet ground. For maximum benefit, select nylon cord in the 160- to 200-pound strength range.

One final lightweight utility to include is a cable saw, with a ring on each end of an 18- to 20-inch saw cable. They can be found in most military surplus stores and are another handy items to have around. ▲

CHAPTER THIRTY-TWO

Tracking Wounded Game

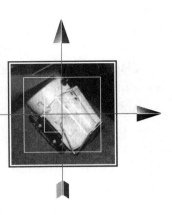

State game agencies set the standards for weapons used for game harvest. If a weapon lacks the power to harvest game humanely, it should not be used. The skill of the hunter is the key to reducing the incidence of crippled game. No hunter wants to injure an animal, but it can happen; a wounded animal somehow manages to disappear into the woods. Real sportsmen dread this, and they work hard to recover it when it happens.

Rifles and ammunition come in a variety of sizes, weights and impact energy. Lightly constructed bullets open on impact but fail to penetrate; the heavier, strongly constructed bullets open only slightly on light, thin-skinned animals. Lighter bullets expand rapidly on impact, leaving large internal damage for a short depth but no exit hole. That often makes it difficult to retrieve the animal. Heavier, stronger bullets are meant for larger, tougher game. Using these bullets on light game typically leaves a small entrance wound, little tissue destruction and a small exit hole. The only good that comes from using heavy bullets on lighter game is their tendency to break major bones. Too many hunters use these bullets mistakenly thinking that they are the best in thick brush.

Both types of bullets leave a poor blood trail and, often, a poor recovery. Using the proper bullet for the game you're hunting minimizes wounding problems and underscores your skills as a rifleman and hunter.

Bowhunters should keep their ears open when around other bowhunters. If they hear about a brand of broadhead that comes apart inside game animals, they should avoid it. Too many replaceable soft-blade broadheads cannot take or hold a cutting edge. They dull on impact and push aside vital organs rather than severing them as sharp cutting edges do.

Shoulder blades protect the windpipe and many arteries and veins that lead to and from the heart and lungs. A properly designed broadhead mounted on the correct shaft can penetrate the shoulder blades on a square hit. You should certainly expect complete penetration on a rib cage hit and the cutting edges should remain sharp. Inexperienced bowhunters can't differentiate between wound channels made by sharp cutting edges and those made by dull ones.

In spite of what some hunters think, heavy bow weight is not required for good penetration. Any compound bow with a draw weight of 50 pounds or more and matched with a balanced, sharp broadhead should do a good job on either whitetail or mule deer; 60 pounds will handle elk; and 70 pounds will take the largest animals — moose and big bear. Sixty pounds and above should handle recurve and longbow hunting needs.

Black and grizzly bear bowhunters should become familiar with the "Game Tracker," a spinning reel-like device with a monofilament line that attaches to the hunting arrow. When the arrow strikes an animal, the spinner will feed up to 1,700 feet of white line. Used with heavier weight arrows, it is accurate up to 35 yards. The line plays out as the animal flees, making it easier to track. Many professional black bear guides ask their clients to use a Game Tracker. Black bears have a tough hide, a layer of fat and a barrel chest that can stop all but the best penetrating arrows. Baited bear are shot at close range, and the monofilament line will indicate whether the animal is down, expediting recovery.

Another new locator is a small, hook-like device that embeds itself into the animal's hide and sends out a signal that can be detected by a receiver up to 200 yards away. Although they haven't reached my area, I have seen them in action but never used one. They are very expensive.

Colored surveyor's tape, especially blaze orange or white, can be a great aid to hunters by marking entry points, blazing trails, tracing game or locating spots they need to find again. Orange is most visible in daylight, and white works well at night, especially in artificial light. Most hardware stores carry the tape. Hunters should mark their stand with a 2- or 3-foot length of tape after shooting at game. That's most important to those using guns, since their game tends to be farther away. Those who think they can drop from a tree and walk to downed game may be in for a surprise. The view changes dramatically just a few yards from the stand, and this is where the surveyor's tape comes in handy.

After marking the stand, study the course for the next 30 to 50 yards, looking for a landmark near the animal. Tie some tape to a tree or bush that's on the course of the bullet and easily spotted from the base of your stand; then tie another piece to the landmark you spotted from the stand. If no landmarks are near the target area, hang tape along the course to the site.

Good sportsmen hope to walk to their downed game; if something goes wrong, they look for a good blood trail that leads to the animal. After field dressing the animal and arranging to bring it home, they collect the tape so as not to clutter the woods.

Bowhunters who shoot "bright arrows" often see the results of their shots. If they miss the actual impact, they can often spot the arrow sticking into the ground after passing through an animal. Note whether it is weaving and unsteady and listen for troubled breathing, an indication that the diaphragm was pierced. Many times you can hear the animal as it goes into shock and hits the ground. If your shot doesn't strike a vital area, retrieve the arrow and mark the spot with tape.

Plan your recovery strategy around the weather. Rain can wash away a blood trail, and wind can dry it up or cover it with leaves. If a storm is coming, you have to start the recovery as soon as possible, not waiting until you find helpers. Mark the trail with tape to give you a course to follow in case the weather forces you to interrupt the tracking.

A fence can yield many clues to the animal's path. Weak ones will attempt to crawl under it or try to jump it. Either way, they are likely to leave clumps of hair. Those that can't get on the other side will hug the fence line as they seek to escape. The most difficult places to track game are watery areas like swamps. Under those

A handle and reflector mounted on a Coleman gasoline lantern.

A rechargeable lantern installed in a pickup truck. You will always have a fully charged light available. Check legality on federal refuges and state wildlife management units.

conditions, look for downed trees and small islands where an animal is likely to seek shelter. Recovery in a wet terrain takes a lot of luck.

Move slowly and deliberately as you look for the game, trying to stay at least 250 yards away. If you see it jump, stop and wait an hour for it to die before resuming the pursuit. Don't move quickly to the site of the jump as that could spook your game into running again. A weakened animal will stay in any area where it feels safe, and that's where you'll find it.

If you enlist some helpers, have them walk abreast from the stand along the course you've marked, glancing backward occasionally. The back of an animal can be hard to spot, but the white belly stands out like a neon sign. A mist of hydrogen peroxide can confirm whether a spot is actually blood. If you've never used peroxide, keep some in the bathroom, and the next time you cut yourself shaving, spray the cut with peroxide; the bubbling reaction positively identifies blood.

Luck plays a part in locating wounded game, but your chances can be improved by proceeding slowly and paying attention. Hair is the most overlooked sign of a passing animal. It is always left at the point of impact of both bullets and arrows. A small amount of hair indicates a square body hit; a larger amount suggests a grazing hit across the back. Generally, dark hair comes from the back and a lighter color is from the chest or stomach areas. The color and amount of hair provide clues to the animal's condition. A large amount of dark hair from an animal that's able to run indicates a slight wound and poor blood trail. Chances are it will escape and recover. A small amount of dark hair indicates a lower body square hit; these are serious wounds that leave a good blood trail and give you a good chance of recovery. Large amounts of white hair accompanied by a good blood trail are signs of damage to the heart, lungs or liver. These animals go down quickly and are recovered near the impact area

Too many hunters concentrate on the blood trail and forget to look for tufts of hair that injured animals leave in tree bark as they flee. It's a clue easily found once you start looking. When you spot lodged hair, mark the spot and continue 30 to 40 yards on course, looking for a foot print or more hair. Spray some peroxide at the ground and watch for bubbling blood. Go in a straight line guided by the tape trail. Your companions should follow on a parallel course. If the trail starts to wander, it means the animal is about to go down. Approach any thicket with care; that's probably where you'll find the game.

Crows, jays and magpies will often spot a wounded animal and give voice. Crows especially seem to have an instinct for spotting them and broadcasting the news. Investigate any unusual activities among the birds in areas near the animal's course.

Many animals are taken in the hour before dark when they increase their activities. If you score and don't hear the animal fall, you are going to need light. I have a buddy who keeps a spotlight in his pickup on a built-in charger. A spotlight can come in handy in many ways, but check the game regulations if you are on a federal refuge or state game management area. A Coleman gasoline lantern equipped with a reflector makes the best track light, I feel, because it never grows dim as battery lights do. The brilliance of the lantern makes blood stand out like diamonds at high noon. Propane lanterns don't have that brilliance.

I have standard procedures for late-evening deer that you might follow. First, return to the vehicle, bringing in the deer stands and bows.

Again, know the game recovery regulations in your state and follow them. Go back to the site of impact and mark it with white tape. Have your companion point the light while you stand 15 to 20 yards behind. As your companion sweeps the area with the light, look for disturbed leaves on low vegetation and on the ground. A spotlight seems to make them stand out. Also check for blood spots and hair lodged in bark. All are clues that make the trail easy to follow.

When following a trail in daylight, look for disturbed vegetation, both on shrubs and the ground. Also check for hair snagged on trees, which means taking your eyes off the ground and observing the overall picture. Again, remember to mark your trail with tape — it can be the most important thing you do.

There are no hard and fast rules about how long you should wait before pursuing a wounded animal, although weather can be a factor. An animal hit in the stomach needs time to expire, but while the wound says "wait," the weather may say "recover." In general, it is better to let a wounded animal expire even if it takes all night and brings a risk of finding a carcass the next morning. In these cases, a short marked trail of about 100 yards can be a big help.

Be cautious with an animal struck in the spine or one that falls immediately from an arrow. Be safe and put another shot through the rib cage.

No one wants an animal to suffer because of a non-fatal wound. Skillful hunting techniques that come from experience can hold game wounding and loss to a minimum. Here are some steps any hunter can take to avoid crippling an animal:

✦ *Go to a "bright arrow." This step heads my list, and I cite their advantages several times in this book.*

✦ *Carry plenty of blaze orange and white tape; it doesn't cost very much, has many uses and fits easily in a fanny pack.*

✦ *Avoid hunting in the rain. While many hunters think a light rain stirs game, it also quickly erases a blood trail.*

✦ *If you see an approaching animal, try to anticipate its course. When it goes behind cover, position yourself for the shot. Say to yourself, "When his head goes behind a tree, I will start my draw, and when he steps out, I'll get him in the rib cage." This type of planning will bring a great improvement in your hunting skills — bow or gun.*

✦ *The most difficult task is learning to keep your mouth shut about wounding and losing a game animal. Sport hunting has enemies who thrive on misinformation and they will use your statement, "I hit him but lost him," against the sport at every opportunity.* ▲

CHAPTER THIRTY-THREE

How Bowhunters Are Injured

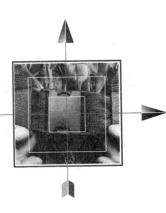

Thanks to the efforts of organized archers and the Game and Fish Commission, the 1995-96 Arkansas bowhunting season was one of its safest. Over the nearly 60 years that the state has permitted bowhunting, there have been but three mistaken-for-deer accidents, one of them fatal. Falls from treestands or treestands that collapse are the leading cause of bowhunting injuries across the U.S. The use of inadequate safety belts — ropes or poorly designed belts that trap a hunter because his weight puts it under too much tension — are the next leading cause. No one has died from using a wrong belt, but many hunters have suffered painful injuries because of them.

A tree climbing aid for a Loggy Bayou. The strap serves as a seat and assist in climbing. It also provides additional safety.

The experience of a young attorney in south-west Arkansas is typical. A recent convert to bowhunting, he headed into the woods even when his usual hunting companion couldn't join him. He climbed a tree, secured himself with a rope and scanned the woods for game. Without warning, the climbing stand collapsed. The lawyer dropped 2 feet before the rope jerked him to a halt, holding him so tightly he could barely breathe. After a two-hour struggle, he managed to grab the tree and cut the rope, only to tumble 15 feet to the ground. Unable to walk, he tried to crawl back to his truck but became mired in a wet ditch.

When the lawyer didn't return home, his wife became concerned and asked his hunting companion for help. Searches of their usual hunting areas proved fruitless, but the companion remembered the new site they had discovered over the weekend. He radioed the sheriff's deputy in that part of the county and soon the hunter's truck was located. Shortly afterward, the hunter himself, cold and shivering in the ditch, was rescued. Brought to safety, the hunter, who happens to be my brother-in-law's lawyer, recovered. As the old saying goes, accidents are loaded with good intentions; in this case, they turned sour rapidly.

Here are the mistakes he made:

1. He went hunting without a companion; if he had felled an animal, there was no way he could get it back without help.

2. He never alerted someone as to the area where he planned to hunt.

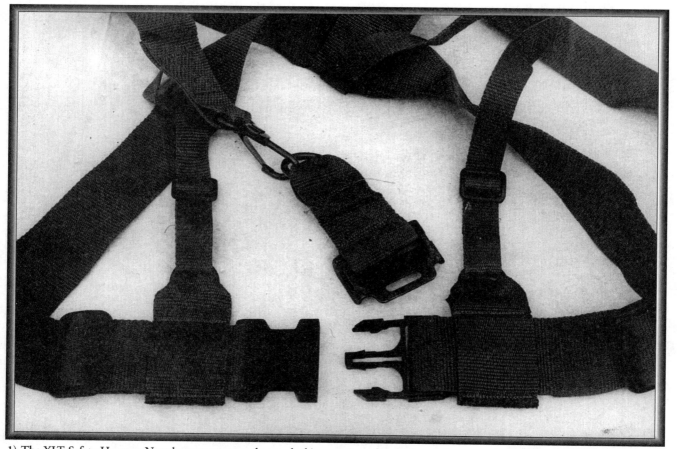

1) The XLT Safety Harness. Note harness snap on the tree locking portion of the belt and the easy to loosen snap for the harness.

2) Preparing to snap the harness.

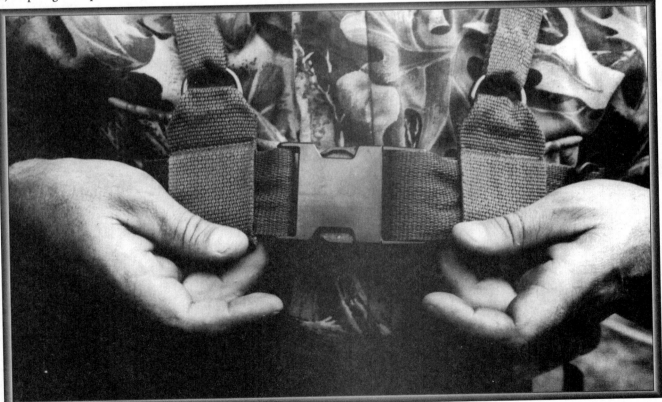

3) The snap is in place. Notice the release cutouts.

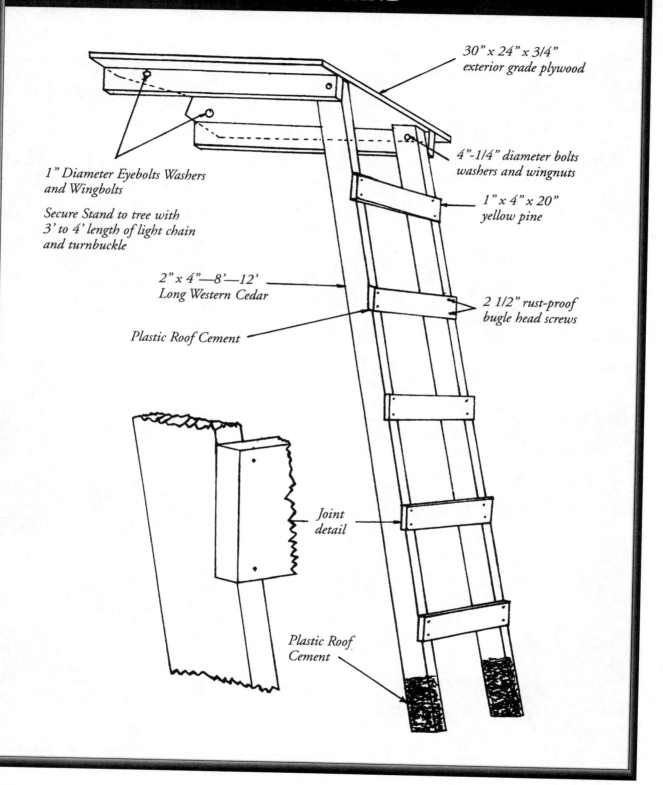

30" x 24" x 3/4"
exterior grade plywood

4"-1/4" diameter bolts
washers and wingnuts

1" x 4" x 20"
yellow pine

2 1/2" rust-proof
bugle head screws

1" Diameter Eyebolts Washers
and Wingbolts

Secure Stand to tree with
3' to 4' length of light chain
and turnbuckle

2" x 4"—8'—12'
Long Western Cedar

Plastic Roof Cement

Joint
detail

Plastic Roof
Cement

Some full equipment practice from the top of an eighteen foot Purdy Widow Maker. Note safety belt.

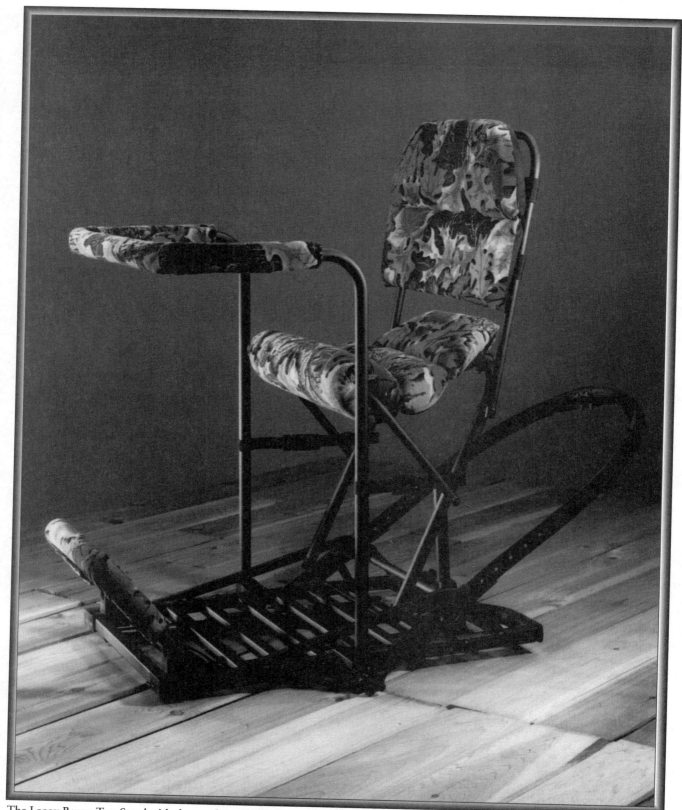

The Loggy Bayou Tree Stand with the comforts of your favorite chair. Courtesy Jenny Bach of Loggy Bayou.

3. He used a slip noose on the rope around his body; a knot like that cannot be loosened while under the tension of the body's weight.

4. He used a treestand that cannot be secured.

Some survival tips the lawyer-hunter should have observed:

1. Keep treestands in top condition.

2. Use a climbing aid with the treestand for the extra protection.

3. Use a nylon rope to pull your bow, arrows and other equipment into the treestand.

4. Know the area where you're hunting and carry a map. If you're going to be in "big woods," bring along a duffel bag with survival gear that includes a 12-foot square of plastic, candles, drinking water, energy bars, mosquito repellent,

A right angle pull on the black strap will free you from the belt or the belt from the tree. Being able to free yourself from a safety belt without taking a fall is important to your health and safety.

Travis uses the Loggy Bayou for a portable stand. Note the riding lawnmower innertube for a cushion.

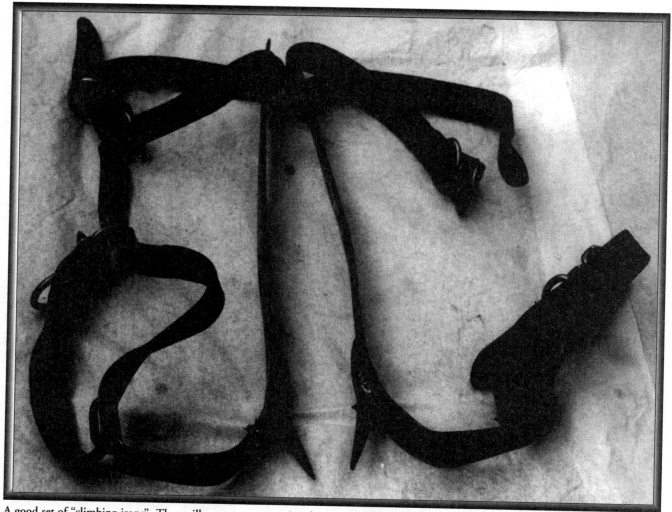

A good set of "climbing irons". They will get you up a tree in a hurry. Check the legality in your state because of bark damage.

a flashlight with extra batteries, a small roll of nylon cord and fire-making equipment. It sounds like a lot, but it's really quite light.

5. Get yourself a geographical positioning system (GPS), or at least a good compass, and learn to use it. Open areas like city parks or small airports are ideal for developing these skills. As you become experienced, your confidence in them — and yourself — will grow. Your camp site or vehicle are the best GPS "go-to" locations, while a baseline spotted on the compass is often the shortest and quickest way out. These have to be established before you go into the woods.

6. Keep your first aid equipment and procedures up to date. For instance, the old "cut-and-suck" snake bite treatment is obsolete as are many other old-time remedies. A small roll of 2-inch gauze, a tube of antibiotic cream and several large adhesive bandages can handle most minor injuries. Remember, though, the farther you'll be from medical assistance, the more first aid equipment you should carry. Judge the distance to medical aid by time, not distance.

7. If someone is injured, return to your vehicle and drive to a location where you can call the nearest emergency room. Report the problem and estimate how long it will take you

to reach the site. If it's a serious injury and you're afraid traffic will slow the recovery, ask for a police car to meet you en route and lead the way. Time can be a life or death factor.

8. You can't depend on luck to get you through an emergency. Survival often depends on adequate training for everyone involved in the hunt.

Accidents can happen anywhere, but the type will vary by location. You're not apt to freeze to death in Florida or suffer a snake bite in Alaska, so prepare for the area where you're headed. Falls from treestands are common among bowhunters, who are also known for cutting or stabbing themselves with broadheads, knives and axes. I have two friends who, on consecutive days, cut their legs with chain saws. They had little experience with the saws, but they learned quickly what not to do.

More serious was the young hunter who climbed a tubular steel ladder and fell asleep. With nothing to hold him in the stand seat, he fell to the ground and is now a quadriplegic. An old bowhuting friend experienced in handling snakes caught a rattler to demonstrate fang erection and venom injection. He was careless and took a fang in the finger. Even though he was near his truck, he was 30 minutes away from medical assistance. He survived the bite, in part because he called from the first phone he

A top quality climbing stand by Billy Fletcher. Bill is a professional welder with the proper equipment and know how. He and his father are also good bowhunters.

saw to have a medical team ready for him. In another case, a member of a Mississippi River hunting club in Arkansas went into anaphylactic shock from a yellow jacket sting. Although there were two doctors in the hunting party, neither had an antidote. The victim had to be taken over two miles of rough terrain and several miles of paved road to reach a hospital. Nearly half an hour after going into shock, the hunter "came back to life," thankful for the wonderful people who literally saved his life. The truth is, I was that hunter, and I didn't think I had much time left on this earth. You can bet that a small syringe of epinephrine goes wherever I go.

Accidents can happen anywhere, usually at the worst time. As they say, "If it can happen, it will." But accidents don't have to happen to you — and they won't if you analyze your outdoor lifestyle, determine the danger areas and eliminate them. That doesn't mean taking a negative attitude about what might happen; it simply means using your common sense. Safe hunting. ▲

The Loggy Bayou Tree Stand shown with climbing aid. (Insert) Courtesy Jenny Bach of Loggy Bayou.

CHAPTER THIRTY-FOUR

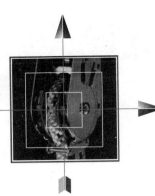

Dressing Your Game

ow many hunters do you know who own the equipment needed for skinning and processing their own game and who take that equipment with them into the woods? How many hunters do you know who have consulted with a taxidermist to improve their skinning and capping skills?

After downing game, your first steps are to verify that it is dead and then declare that the animal is legally yours. State requirements vary, but marking your license typically allows you to remove the animal's intestines and take it to a check station. Having the equipment to field dress an animal shows that you have confidence in your hunting ability. Kenny Oldham, Ben Pearson's guide on his polar beat hunt, said he had 30 minutes or less to remove the head and hide from a trophy bear before it froze. You can

Dale Halbrook displaying his skill as a taxidermist. Courtesy of Dale Halbrook

How To Butcher Your "Critter"

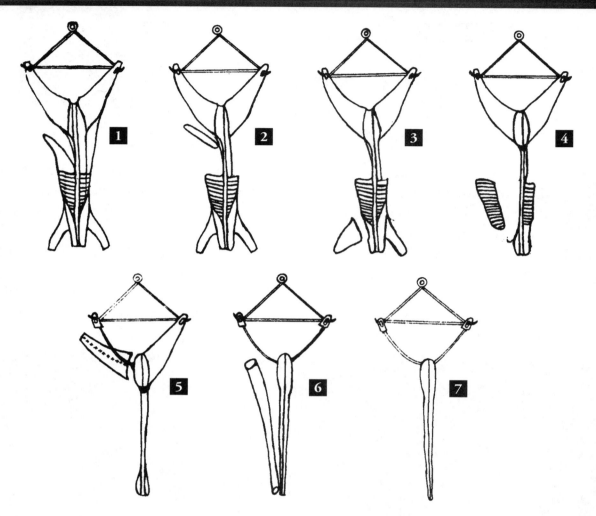

1. The skinned carcass showing removal of the thin flank tissue.

2. Removal of the "Tenders" from the underside of the backbone.

3. Removing the shoulders.

4. Use bone saw to remove each side of the ribcage.

5. Follow outside contour of hip bones with a thin bladed knife. Follow leg bones from hip plates to tendon joints. This step debones the hams.

6. Use a short bladed knife. Follow each side of a thin ridge on top of the backbone. Debone each backstrap from the rump to the end of the neck. Cut into lengths equal to a strip of bacon or crossways into one half inch thick ministeaks for frying.

7. All that is left is backbone, hip plates, leg bones, and tendon joints. Now the head, feet, and intestines is just about what the "Old Pioneers" left in the woods to feed the opossums.

8. Place your meat in a ice chest or chests and pack with ice cubes. Drain daily for three days then wrap for the freezer.

bet that his knife and saw were handy and sharp before the hunt began.

Talk to a local taxidermist about caping game. If possible, spend some time with him as he works. It's likely he would rather show you basic caping and cape preservation skills than to explain why your trophy mount looks so terrible. It takes a good cape to produce a quality mount. Splitting the hide in the direction of the hair growth leaves much less hair on the carcass after skinning. Palm the knife so that your fingers protect against accidentally puncturing the intestines as you split the hide and stomach membrane. Cutting the intestines can foul the carcass.

Ask the local wildlife agency whether a liver disease is common among game in the area and whether it is safe to eat. The liver is often the first internal organ to show signs of illness. Game liver and heart are considered delicacies; learning to avoid problems means eating a prime meal without worry.

The tools needed for skinning and butchering are inexpensive and widely available. Here's what you'll need (all of which can be easily carried in a pickup's tool box):

✦ *A package of disposable thin latex gloves. They'll protect you from infections by eliminating contact with the intestines and stomach. These gloves can be found at pharmacies and most sporting goods stores.*

✦ *A good knife with a drop point blade that is no longer than 5 inches. Use it on hide and flesh, but not on bone. A knife that can't hold its sharpness while gutting, skinning and butchering is either made of low quality steel or was used previously to cut or chop bone. You will need a good knife each time you go into the woods, so buy the best you can afford; it's a lifetime investment. Keep a sharpening kit or a hone at the camp so your knife is always ready.*

These knives handle our caping, skinning, and dressing.

- *A hacksaw frame and a bone-cutting blade between 12 and 14 inches long. These saws should come apart for easy storage and transportation.*
- *A gambrel — a device for hanging game — can be purchased from a sporting goods store or through its catalogs. I keep a gambrel, meat saw and a small block and tackle to lift the carcass for skinning and butchering. This equipment is also used for rotating elk and moose for easier access to the pelvic and stomach areas.*
- *A 48-quart ice chest. It can hold a boned deer and up to three bags of ice cubes.*
- *On extended pack trips away from automotive transportation — into the Rocky Mountain high country, for instance — bring several yards of cheese cloth or mosquito netting to wrap the meat while it's suspended. Sprinkle black pepper generously on the meat before and after wrapping it with the netting to keep flies away. Hang the meat in shade and protect it from dew and other moisture. High altitudes are usually cool enough to delay spoilage a few days, but keep a close check.*
- *To prevent spoilage, use plain (not iodized) table salt to cover the hide and cape after fleshing.*
- *Have a box of heavy-duty plastic bags handy for carrying the boned meat for disposing the refuse. Make sure the bags are unscented — the odor can ruin the taste of the meat.*

Because our nation's pioneers depended on game for food, they dressed their kill on the spot. Today's hunters say that pioneers took only preferred cuts with them, but since they hunted on foot they had little choice. They left the bones and fat. If the hide was needed for clothing and they couldn't lug it all out at once, the hunter would make a return trip.

The hunting habits of the pioneer are worth emulating. He first checked the animal for signs

A well organized meat house.

CAPING CUTS TO PREPARE
YOUR TROPHY FOR THE TAXIDERMIST

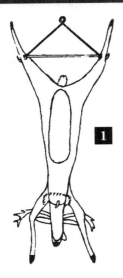

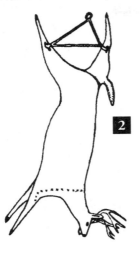

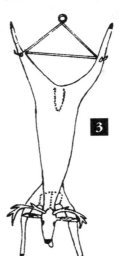

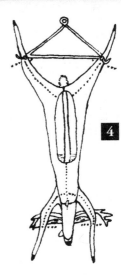

The Shoulder Mount

Skinning Cuts

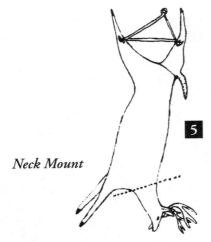

Neck Mount

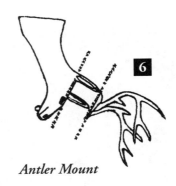

Antler Mount

1. Shows hide cut across the bottom of the chest, up and forward the inside of the leg area.

2. Side view shows hide cut coming around the front legs, then extending back and up the chest meeting at the top of the backbone

3. Hide cut extending up the top of the neck and making a short "Y" joining and going around each antler burr.

4. Hide cuts needed for a simple skinning.

5. One of two cuts for a neck mount. The second cut is a cut on top of the neck joining the antler burr. See **3**.

6. Shows skull cap containing the antlers being remover from the head. This is a straight cut using a bone saw.

of life. If its eyes were closed, but the rib cage was still moving, he would cut its throat (gun powder and lead were too valuable to waste). If the animal's eyes were open, he would touch an eye ball with a small stick. Rather than cut the animal's throat, the modern hunter should shoot the animal through the neck bone (unless he plans to mount it, in which case, he should shoot the animal through the heart from several feet away to allow for movement.

After verifying that the animal is dead, roll it onto its back and slip the point of the knife under the skin at the sternum and split the skin over the stomach pouch. Continue cutting along both sides of the sex organ and circle the anus. Shielding the knife point between your fingers, carefully cut the stomach membrane, pushing the intestines out of the way. If you have a meat saw, split the sternum until the saw hits the

lungs. Locate the bladder and tie off the urinary canal with string to prevent urine from spilling into the body cavity. Free the intestines by cutting the urinary canal, diaphragm and windpipe. If the colon and anus did not drop out of the carcass, leave the pelvic plate intact

When you reach the skinning site, saw the pelvic plate and clean it. If the liver is in good condition, save it and the heart for the evening meal. Be sure to comply with game registration rules before skinning. Hook the gambrel around the large tendon just below the knee. Hoist the animal and make cuts encircling all four legs at the knees.

Shoulder Mount

Now comes the big decision: Are you going to have the animal mounted? For a shoulder mount, start your cut at the top of the backbone — about 8 inches from where it joins the neck

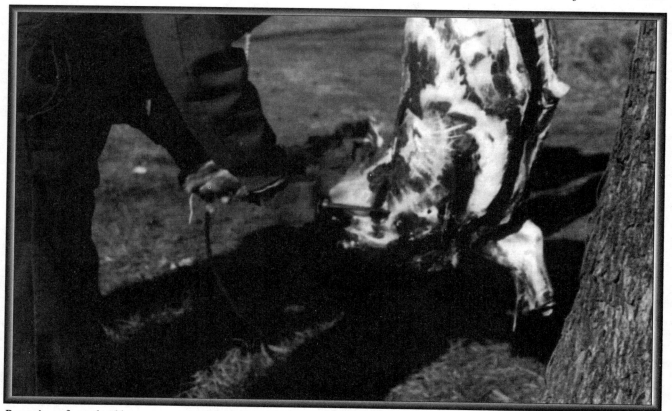

Removing a front shoulder

Removing the rib cage with a meat saw

— and continue down the rib cage to just in front of the shoulder. Make the next cut around the outside of the shoulder ham from front to back. Run the next cut up the inside of the ham as far as the rib cage, then across the sternum, joining a similar cut on the other side, encircling the chest. Start the next cut on top of the neck bone about an inch behind the antler spurs. Run the cut down the top of the spine until it meets the cuts that encircle the body. Make two short cuts to connect to the antler burrs. These cuts were made to remove the cape, but hold off on this until the head is severed and the rear portion of the animal has been skinned. By waiting, you protect the meat from falling hair during the skinning process. After removing the hide from the body and hindquarters, start working the cape free of the animal. Use the saw to sever the head 5 or 6 inches behind the ear. Lay the head and cape on a work table and finish the butchering.

Neck Mount

Neck mounts are frequently shoulder mounts gone bad — perhaps the taxidermist didn't have enough cape to do the job right. If the rack is large, you may try to get a cape from other kills in the camp. You can also wait until your next kill. A large, well-proportioned rack deserves an attractive mount. A neck mount is less expensive and is often selected for the first deer bagged by a younger member of the family.

For a neck mount, make the first cut from the top of the backbone and encircle the front of the chest. Make another cut starting about an inch from the antler burrs running down the top of the neck bone until it reaches the top of the chest cut. Leave the cape in place until you finishing skinning the rear portion.

Protecting the intestines with two fingers while opening the body cavity.

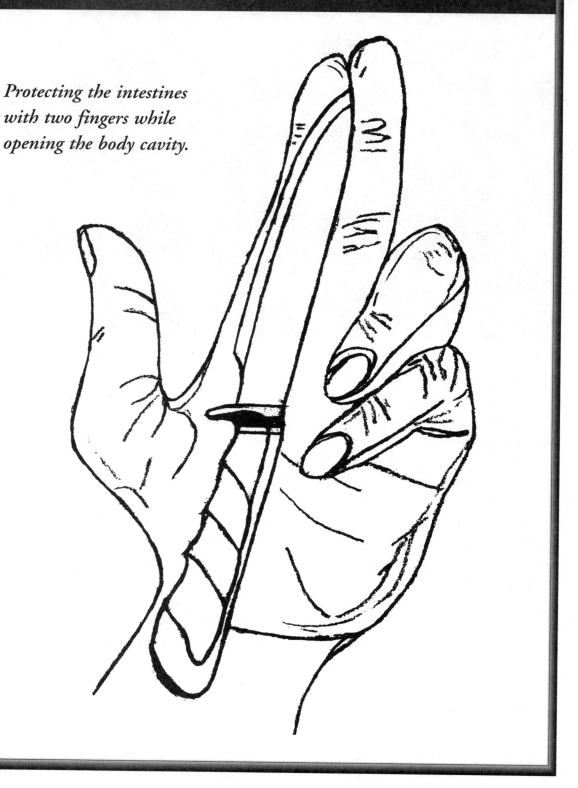

The Antler Mount

Place the saw blade in a flat position just ahead of the ears and cut forward under the antler burrs. Pass across the top of the eye sockets and exit the skull. Peel the skin from the antler plate and clean out the brain cavity. The antler skull will be moist, so dry it with a coat of plain table salt.

Many sporting goods stores stock antler mount boards and kits that include a velvet covering to complete the presentation. One of the best things about an antler mount is the ease of cleaning. Apply a coat of thinned linseed oil to retain the shine of the antlers. With the mounting decision out of the way, it's time to get on with the skinning and butchering. Many people will handle this for a nominal fee; but doing it yourself produces the best-tasting venison. A deer is not a steer, so don't butcher it as you would with beef. Power saws used by professional beef butchers get coated when used on venison, giving the meat a gummy taste. With deer, it's best to do as the pioneers did.

To remove the skin, split it from the throat to the opening at the sternum. Resume the cut at the pelvic plate and circle the anus. From here, cut up the inside of each leg, encircling each leg at the start of the foreleg. Cut the tail bone and start pulling the hide from the body and from each leg. If you don't plan a neck or shoulder mount, complete skinning the neck. Sever the head with the saw and pull off the hide, cutting it from the neck and head. Use the saw to cut off the forelegs. Remove the thin stomach membrane. Starting at the pelvic area, follow the backbone to the rear rib and take out the second membrane (use two pieces of membrane in your next batch of chili).

Removing the thin flank tissue

The "Power Ratchet", a handy tool to elevate or roll a heavy carcass over. Courtesy Hawk Assoc. and Carolina North MFG. Co.

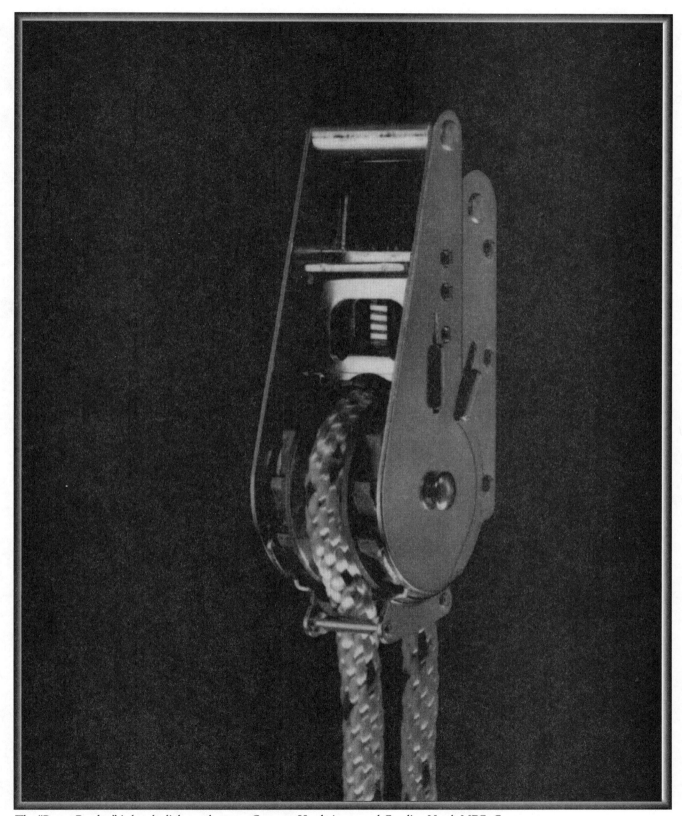

The "Power Ratchet" is handy, light, and strong. Courtesy Hawk Assoc. and Carolina North MFG. Co.

Remove one of the front shoulders by cutting upward and pulling the hams outward until they separate from the joint and rib cage. Repeat the process on the other shoulder. Cook them in an oven and apply a good barbecue sauce. The shoulder bone and shoulder blade are very difficult to bone. Use a saw to remove the rib cage, cutting just under the backbone and working forward, severing each rib. Boning is impractical, so pop them in the over with plenty of barbecue sauce.

Using your knife, make parallel cuts on each side of the center of the spine the length of the carcass, from the rump to the neck. These two pieces are called "backstraps," which I cut into strips the length of bacon. My wife pins two or three strips of bacon to each piece of backstrap just before broiling them. Keeping things in the family, my son Rayburn prefers to cut around the

outside of the hip bone plate to the thigh bone, pulling the meat from the bone and hanging it from the gambrel. If you have a butcher friend, try to talk him out of a few feet of butcher twine to make a bone-free rolled roast. It's venison at its best.

Pioneers carried home the best of the deer and so will you. Put the cut up deer in the ice chest and cover it with ice cubes. After 24 hours, drain the bloody water and add more ice. Repeat the process after another 24 hours, and once again the next day. The meat is then ready for freezing. While the meat is soaking in the ice chest, go back to work on the capes and hides. Remove the head from the cape, using a stainless steel spoon to separate the hide from the flesh inside the ears. Use the spaying blade of a pocket knife to work the cape from around the eyes and lips. When you've finished fleshing, apply a

Travis' carport displays some of his successful hunts.

Skinning out a "buck tail" to make fishing flies

Standard equipment on my trips to deer camp

generous amount of plain salt to remove the moisture and set the hair.

We use generous amounts of plastic wrap on the meat before freezing it. If there's any possibility that some air can leak into the package, add another layer. Seal it tightly with freezer tape. Don't try to save a few pennies by using masking tape — it can loosen in the freezer. Use a moisture-resistant pen to indicate the type of meat and date on the package.

It takes a thorough fleshing to preserve a hide. Salting a green, fleshy hide won't protect it during shipment to the tannery. If you're stuck with the job, use a stainless steel spoon as a scraper. Put the hide on a flat surface with the flesh side up and work the flesh off. If you're lucky, you might find someone who buys green cow hides and has a fleshing machine.

After fleshing, apply a generous coating of plain salt before rolling the hide for shipment to a tannery or to a business that specializes in making buckskin garments. Wrap the green hide in a plastic bag and seal it inside a cardboard box. *Don't ever wrap a hide — green or tanned — in newspaper; the ink can penetrate a green hide and stain a tanned one.*

The meat is in the freezer, the cape and antlers are at the taxidermist and the hide is salted and on its way to the tannery. When they all come back, there's more cleaning to do. Use a vacuum cleaner wherever you find hair. Don't use oils or chemicals, which can saturate hair follicles and cause the hair to fall out. Clean the glass eyes with a soft cotton swab, and use a medium width paint brush barely moistened with thinned linseed oil on the antlers. All these precautions can keep your good looking trophy looking good! ▲

CHAPTER THIRTY-FIVE

Sharpening

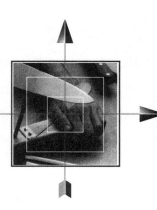

y father taught me the art of sharpening a knife when I was a small lad, impressing on me that the only sharpening stones worthy of a good blade were processed from the natural sharpening material found and finished near Hot Springs, Arkansas. They are called "Ouachita" or "Arkansas" stones, depending on their grit.

The stone should be lubricated to keep its pores from filling with the material removed during sharpening. Dad insisted that only water be used, swiping the stone with a wet rag before the next sharpening. High-carbon steel blades and water make a good sharpening combination. Using oil on a stone can contaminate the blade, making it unsuitable for preparing food. A butcher I once knew would not allow knives

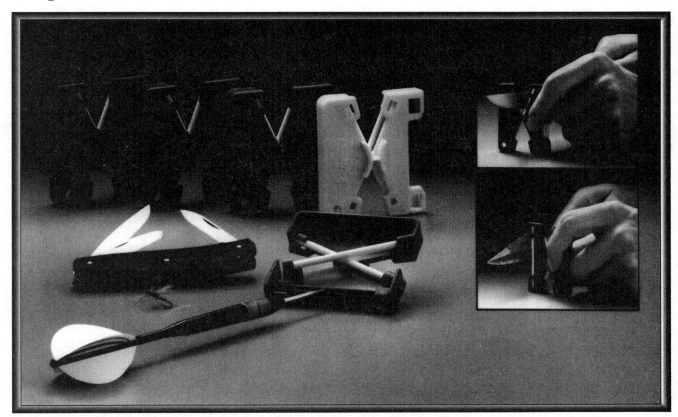

A small pocket sized Gatco unit for small knives, broadheads, etc. Courtesy Gatco.

GENERAL SHARPENING RULES

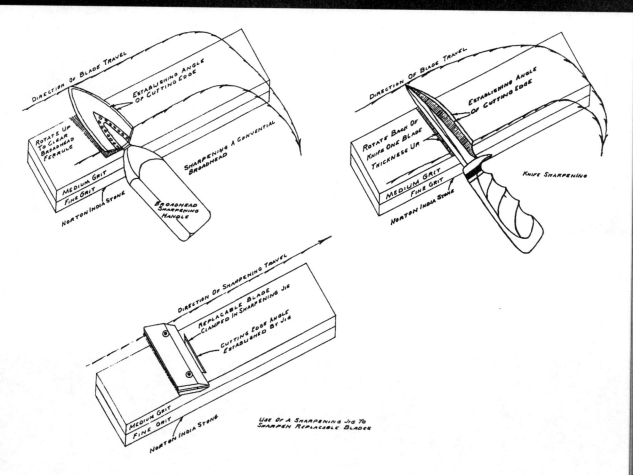

1. *Use a holding handle when sharpening screw-in broadheads.*

----

2. *Use a holding jig or clamp when sharpening replaceable broadhead blades.*

----

3. *Permanently attached broadheads 2-3-4 fixed blades are often sharpened easier by use of a Gatco, EZE-Lap or Muzzy sharpening devices. Remember sharpening a broadhead attached to an arrowshaft demands caution.*

----

4. *Use a holding device when sharpening anything.*

----

5. *Use a protection device to protect your finely honed cutting edge.*

----

6. *Use an approved honing oil where applicable.*

into his shop that had been sharpened on an oiled stone. Rather, he used salt brine to lubricate his sharpening stones. Years later, an old machinist gave me a Norton India bench stone, a combination medium-fine grit oil stone that soon became one of my favorites.

I recently learned of a system for sharpening tools manufactured by the Great American Tool Company and marketed under the GATCO name. The system has re-educated me about the best way to sharpen anything. One GATCO tool offers angle adjustments that tailor it to the tool's use. For instance, a shallow angle gives a hide-popping edge for skinning and cutting meat.

Increase the angle for knives carried on belts and used to cut limbs, rope, shaving for fire starting and field dressing where opening the pelvic cavity and chest areas are possibilities. An ax or hatchet used for cutting firewood needs an even steeper edge. It's a good idea to use a saw for tough cutting jobs around the camp, saving the knives for the woods and field. The GATCO tool puts on the desired cutting edge mush faster than the old bench stones put on a hand-held blade.

GATCO offers a ceramic device small enough to fit in a shirt pocket that can sweeten the edge of a knife used for field dressing or skinning. A

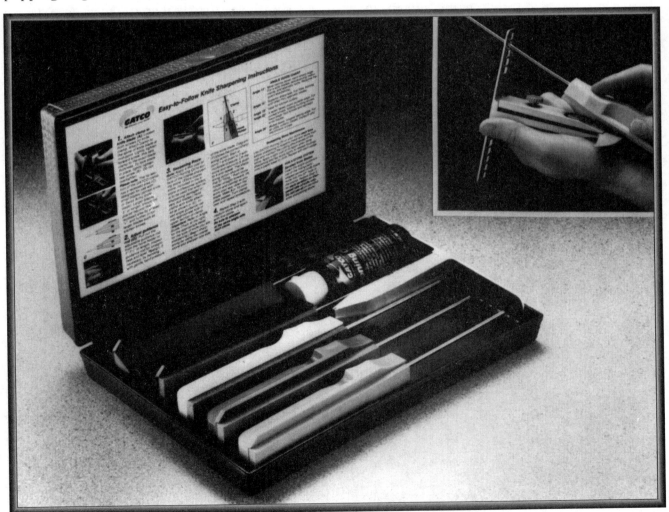

A Gatco Knife Sharpening Hone. This tool sets the angle for a good cutting edge. Courtesy Gatco.

larger set of ceramic sticks is designed to safely keep household knives sharp. I suspect that somewhere in the GATCO sharpening system there is a way to put an edge on a bowling ball. The company's approach to sharpening impresses me.

Too many of today's hunters never learned proper sharpening techniques. The first step is to start with a good brand of knife. My sons and I usually carry Schrade, Buck or Gerber lock blades, which range from inexpensive to real money. Hand-made custom knives sometimes look better, cost much more money and hold an edge a little longer, but they, too, have to be sharpened. For good sharpening, invest in a Norton India dual grit bench stone, medium-coarse on one side and fine on the other. At the same time, get a small bottle of a name-brand honing oil that's been approved by the U.S. Food and Drug Administration. The days of the "water-only lube" went out with the development of lubes based on light white mineral oils. Additionally, stainless steel blades require a modern sharpening lubrication.

The following steps explain and illustrate how to hone a cutting edge.

✦ *Place the stone on a thick folded cloth at the end of a table.*

✦ *Lay the blade flat on the surface of the stone. Rotate the blade 90 degrees, placing the dulled edge in direct contact with the stone. You have positioned your blade from one extreme to the other. If you tried to sharpen the blade in the flat position, it would take hours of hand labor that would eventually produce a thin, keen edge. Because the knife lacks sufficient steel backing, it*

The sharpening jig detailed in this book shown holding a replaceable broadhead blade.

Construction Instructions

1. Cut the flatstock into two equal lengths 2 3/8" long.

2. Sandwich the shimstock between the flatstock and drill a 1/16" diameter hold thru the flatstock and shimstock.

3. Tap the bottom piece of flatstock with a No. 1x72 tap.

4. Clearance drill the top piece of flatstock and shimstock with a No. 48 drill.

5. Countersink the top piece of flatstock for screwhead clearance.

6. Use one screw to clamp everything together while you tap drill, clearance drill, and countersink the other end of your work.

7. Bevel the edges of the top and bottom flatstock. Using a grinding wheel helps to expedite the shaping of the bevels but finish the job with a small flat file.

8. Scribe the outline of a replaceable blade onto the shimstock so the dulled edge projects out about one-eighth of an inch. Trim out the scribbed area with scissors. Now solder the shimstock to the bottom piece of flatstock. The shimstock cut-out should automatically position a dull blade inserted in the jig for sharpening.

9. A few strokes on a fine grit stone should prepare a dulled blade for a super finish on a hard stone. After all isn't super performance from you and your equipment the bottom line in bow hunting.

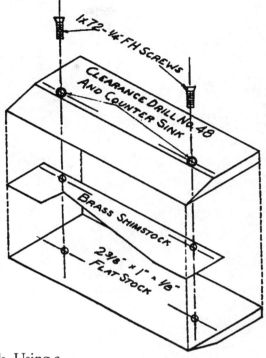

Required Materials

1. One piece steel flatstock 1" x 5" x 1/8".

2. One piece brass shimstock 5/8" x 2 3/8" .006" to .008" thick.

3. Two flathead screws No. 1x72-1/4" long.

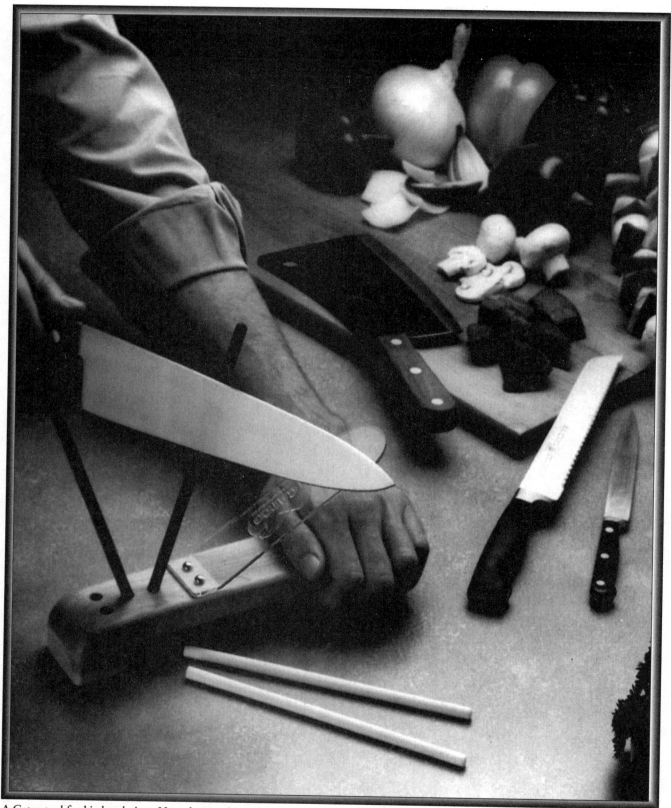

A Gatco tool for kitchen knives. Note the guard to give your wife a secure feeling while sharpening. Courtesy Gatco.

Hunting And Shooting With The Modern Bow

would lose it sharpness in a few strokes. A surgeon might appreciate such an edge, but a woodsman only cusses out a knife that won't stay sharp.

✦ Stand the blade on its cutting edge. Pull it back and forth on its dull edge to eliminate nicks and true an uneven edge left by someone not skilled in sharpening. Place the blade perpendicular to the stone and pull it from hilt to tip. A few strokes usually corrects an abused edge. To judge your progress, point the blade toward a light bulb, which will highlight remaining spots and nicks. A uniform reflected edge tells you to proceed to the next step.

✦ You now have a very dull but nick-free blade ready for correct sharpening. Sprinkle several drops of honing oil on the medium grit side of the stone. Lay the blade on the stone with the point trailing the hilt by about 15 degrees. Raise the back edge of the blade until you have a gap equal to the thickness of the blade back. Maintain this tip drag and blade gap as you start pushing the blade straight toward the far end of the stone. At 5 inches, start pulling the hilt away from the stone, dragging the tip across the stone and exiting during the last inches of forward and outward travel.

✦ Turn the blade over and duplicate the gap and training tip angle as you pull it toward you. Be patient: emphasize blade gap and tip drag. Keep repeating these steps. Don't be in a rush; you'll gain speed as you become more experienced. Check the blade, looking for a reasonably uniform strip of fresh metal along both sides of the cutting edge from hilt to tip. When the edge seems to disappear, it is time to change to the fine grit stone.

The dual grit Norton India stone will produce a good sharp edge. The coarse grit side establishes cutting angles with little effort. The

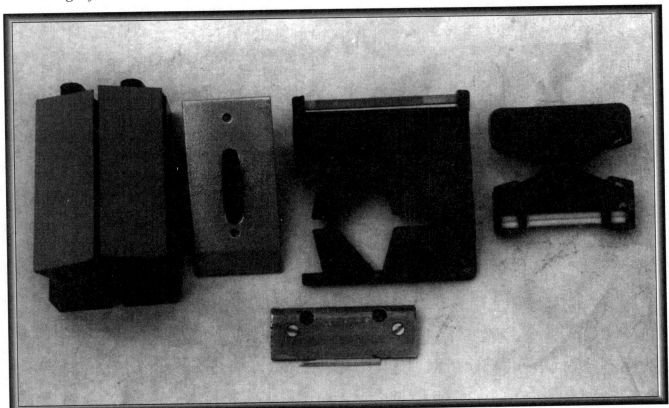

Broadhead Sharpening Jigs (L-R) By Muzzy, Fine Line, EZE Lap, Gatco, and the jig detailed in this book.

fine grit side produces a good, sharp edge. The one-blade thickness gap will provide a long-lasting, working edge that stays sharp for tough cutting jobs. Be content in learning how to develop a keener, hide-popping edge as your skill increases.

✦ *Always support or hold the object to be sharpened with a handle, jig or other device.*

✦ *Whenever possible, support the stone on something solid.*

✦ *Use a stone lubricant that has U.S. Food and Drug Administration approval. Light mineral oil will do a good job. Water works in a jam. Always use some lubrication on a natural stone.*

✦ *Don't allow yourself to be interrupted while sharpening; inattention can lead to a nasty cut.*

✦ *Use a knife for hide and meat, a saw to cut bone, and a wood-cutting saw or ax on wood.*

I have talked about the old and new ways of honing a cutting edge. I hope you've been persuaded that today's outdoorsman needs sharpening know-how as much as did Daniel Boone. I look down on any bowhunter who takes dull equipment into the woods, be it broadheads or a knife. Why go hunting and not take the equipment necessary to care for the game that you've harvested? The tool box in my four-by-four has a gambrel, a lightweight rope hoist and a 14-inch bone saw. Behind the seat is a box of heavyweight plastic bags to carry out the remains of game processing.

Broadheads, replaceable blades and knives should be sharpened at home. If you plan to stay in the woods for several days, add a GATCO diamond hone or a Norton India stone to your tool box and put a GATCO ceramic sharpener or Diamond broadhead sharpener in your quiver or shirt pocket. These small, light devices can handle a lot of sharpening and won't get in the way.

Sharp edges should be protected. Dropping unprotected broadhead arrows into a quiver is not a good idea. I'm jut old-fashioned enough to use an over-the-shoulder back quiver that carries many of the things a bowhunter needs. A number of years ago, a company produced a line of plastic broadhead protectors, but it has since disappeared, leaving only Bear Archery's protectors for its line of Razorheads. I shoot a three-bladed point, which condemns me to using a paper towel and a rubber band.

This warning is worth repeating: If you are going to sharpen something, use a handle or other method to hold the blade securely. And do refer to the drawings in this chapter.   ▲

CHAPTER THIRTY-SIX

Game Management

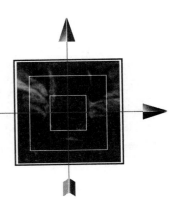

s the 19th century rolled into the 20th, the wildlife population of the United States was at an all-time low. Uncounted herds of buffalo had been shot nearly to extinction; uncontrolled shooting of deer by market hunters left them nearly nonexistent in several central and eastern states. Western mule deer and elk suffered a similar fate. Worse was the attitude of too many people who regarded wildlife as fair game anytime they wanted it. "The Great Slaughter," as it was called, prompted men like President Theodore Roosevelt to spearhead a national conservation movement. Game and fish agencies gained new respect, enabling them to protect and restore the nation's wildlife, despite interference from politicians.

As the 20th century opened, more states adopted game laws, while game refuges were established with funding from the states and the federal government. Today, most game management funding comes from sportsmen; about 75 percent of the states use money from hunting and fishing licenses and permits to pay for their fish and game agencies. Twenty-five percent of the states designate a portion of their sales tax revenue to pay for non-licensed activities that game and fish agencies supervise. Agencies have access to federal money for approved projects under the Dingel-Johnson Act (which was augmented by the Pittman-Robertson Act). Dingle-Johnson requires manufacturers of most sport fishing equipment to put 10 percent of what it costs to make the product into a fund matched by federal government on a three-for-one ratio. Items that carry the 10 percent excise tax under Pittman-Robertson include guns, ammunition, archery equipment and hand guns. Bows and arrows weren't included when the act was adopted in 1937 because archery was then considered a target sport. As the sport grew in popularity after World War II, both target and bowhunters asked Congress to include them under Pittman-Robertson.

Money collected by the surtax is returned to the states under a formula that takes into account the number of licensed hunters that uses its land area. The funds cover about three-fourths of state-initiated but federally approved projects. Since 1937, the program has provided more than $1 billion to restore and propagate harvestable and non-game wildlife. The U.S. Fish and Wildlife Service administers the money through special "pay-as-you-go" funds; none of it comes from other tax sources. Today's sports hunters and fishermen pay their own way.

By the start of World War II, the game protection program was well established and accepted as a way to restore the nation's wildlife.

When the waterfowl population began to dwindle, the United States and Canada joined in a treaty to protect them. U.S. sportsmen formed "Ducks Unlimited" and a similar organization was created in Canada. There are more geese on the North American continent today than ever before; and, because of overpopulation, the duck season was recently extended to 50 days along with an increase in bag limits.

Americans have had a change of mind about their wildlife. Opinions of wildlife biologists carry more weight, and they have more freedom to do their jobs. Game law violations carry heavy penalties, including fines, penalties to cover the loss of wildlife destroyed, loss of hunting privileges and possible prison terms. The laws have greatly reduced the incidence of illegal hunting. Moreover, the public is beginning to realize the importance of an abundant wildlife to the nation, acknowledging the wisdom of scientists who see wildlife as a barometer of the environment. As they go, we go.

Money talks, and when it comes to hunters, it speaks loud and clear. My home state of Arkansas has a relatively small population and its per capita income is not among the highest; but state figures show that in 1994 sport hunters and fishermen spent $588 million to hunt and fish and buy the equipment. Those hobbies provide jobs for about 9,000 people. Arkansas residents spend about $188 million every year to count birds, watch eagles and listen to elk bugle on the Buffalo National River. North Arkansas is covered with trails that attract hikers during the warmer months. They buy binoculars, bird seed, humming bird feeders, gasoline, food , clothing, boots and anything else they feel they need to pursue their hobbies, including renting motel rooms. Arkansas residents are outdoor oriented, taking advantage of the activities sponsored or regulated by the Game and Fish Commission. Most of the money for these activities comes from sport hunting and fishing funds, which support all kinds of wildlife activities.

When you purchased your bow, you declared yourself a candidate for recognition among hunting's elite, and you automatically assumed a responsibility to do your share to preserve wildlife and the environment. Your next step should be to join a local archery club and take an active role. As your skill improves, make yourself available to those less experienced. Volunteer to work with local Boy Scouts. You'll find they appreciate having skilled people working with them on archery projects.

As your skills increase and you become a successful bowhunter, you'll earn the respect of club members who may consider you for a leadership role. Accept it and endeavor to serve well. Once elected, introduce yourself to the local wildlife officer, explaining that you are an official of the local archery club. Give him your name and telephone number and ask that he notify you of any bowhunting problems in the area that you might stop them from spreading or eliminate completely. You won't take part in enforcement actions, but you can help reduce trespassing and assist in game registration, game counts and other programs that benefit wildlife. Don't be surprised if the wildlife officer asks you teach him how to shoot with a bow and arrow, or to bring him up to date on the latest in archery equipment.

Should the time come when you or your entire club want a change in game regulations; the local wildlife officer might be able to help. If there is merit to the request, he can contact a professional biologist for advice on how to pursue the proposal. Prepare the request in writing, choose your words carefully and make sure there are no errors. The final form should be typed neatly, with no corrections. You can expect to appear before those who will decide the fate of your request. Know the pros and cons of your proposal and be prepared to answer questions about it. Make the presentation short and to the point, concluding with a word of thanks for the wildlife officer who helped you with the request. Your statement demonstrates that you've had professional assistance, and it gives the board an opportunity to talk to a professional who can answer their questions. You've just taken a big step toward getting your request approved.

While politicians no longer try to impose their wildlife theories on hunters, they would like to get their hands on the money generated by outdoors people. While only 14 percent of the U.S. population hunts, and a slightly larger number fishes (there is some overlap), the money they generate for all types of wildlife is considerable and has been spent wisely. The whitetail deer herd has grown beyond what could have been imagined 50 years ago. The number of mule deer in western states has reached an all-time high. Elk also flourish in a number of areas (they're so numerous in Arkansas that a controlled harvest is under

Bill Hogue shows his Holla Bend Buck. More sporting good tax dollars working for sportsmen and wildlife.

consideration). The restoration of black bear in Arkansas is considered the most successful restocking of large game animals anywhere. Antelope and Wyoming moose are doing well, too. Game management works, and its benefits are enjoyed everywhere.

People opposed to hunting have not been idle. They persuaded California to pass a mountain lion protection act. Now the animals are so numerous that two or three attacks on humans are reported each year. This somehow gives satisfaction to anti-hunting forces who think the lions are merely doing what comes naturally. The no-dog, no-bait black bear laws recently passed in several western states have brought their numbers to the highest level yet. Black bears can pose problems not easily nor cheaply solved. During a recent summer, some friends in a Rocky Mountain state asked me for advice on dealing with an overly friendly bear. They also have elk and mule deer in their garden, but they eat and run. The bear, however, eats and hangs around, showing little fear of humans. People who have lived under these "be-kind-to-animals" laws have learned the truth about game management the hard way and are working to have the regulations repealed. Sports hunters have a stake in every state's game laws.

The man passing out the score cards is Tom White. His father and I were members of the same Mississippi River Island Deer Club. Tom grew up on this island learning the skills of a hunter. Today he is serving his first term as president of the Arkansas Bowhunter's Association.

Your knowledge of game management and your leadership are needed.

Many people in this country get whatever "education" they have about wildlife from Disney movies and the Discovery channel, which give them a warped idea about wild animals and sport hunting. One of their beliefs is that sport hunting is unnecessary and that wild animals would be just fine without it; they ignore the evidence of game management's success. If hunting and fishing were stopped, where would the money come from to manage and protect wildlife?

The Place Where I Live

The White River flows through southeastern Arkansas, emptying into the Mississippi. The lower portion runs through thousands of acres of giant oak, rock elm and other trees. They were never harvested and formed a canopy that shaded all the undergrowth. The forest was home to squirrels and, in the fall, it supported millions of ducks on their way south. I have many relatives and friends in the area and was fortunate to accompany my father on squirrel and duck hunts there. During the mid-1930s, the U.S. Fish and Wildlife Service purchased about 155,000 acres of the land as a waterfowl refuge. To fund the acquisition, Congress ordered that the timber be harvested (in those days, Congress believed in paying for what it spent). The four counties surrounding the purchase area realized they could lose money, and it was agreed they would share in the proceeds. It was a wise move; in 1995, the counties received $494,000 from the annual timber harvest.

With some trees cleared by the first harvest, light reached the ground, encouraging the growth of brush as thickets — a phenomenon

soon recognized by deer further down the Mississippi. During the summer of 1945, the late G.T. Alter of De Witt, Arkansas, took his son, Charles, Bill Clements and me to a refuge lake where Alter pointed out a deer track. Ten years later, we found tracks there from an entire herd who figured they had found "deer heaven." They could not be hunted, and they faced no natural enemies. All they had to do was eat and multiply.

Those who arranged the purchase failed to take into account the annual spring flooding of the lowlands where the White River joins the Mississippi, forcing the deer onto adjoining agricultural land. Farmers who faced ruin as hungry deer devoured their crops took their pleas to their local governments, game officials and anyone else they thought could help. Gaming officials suggested that farmers be allowed to shoot the deer as long as the animals were butchered by game officers and the meat given to charitable institutions. Health officials nixed that idea, though, saying the butchering would not be done under sanitary condition. Well, then, said the game officials, shoot the deer and let the carcasses lie there and rot.

Soon rifle fire echoed throughout the area as farmers took steps to protect their crops. Tempers flared and ugly words were exchanged, straining relationships between farmers who lived next to the refuge and those further removed.

In 1958, a major die-off of deer struck the lower part of the refuge. Friends told me they spotted 28 dead deer from along the roadside during a three-mile drive into the refuge. In 1961, a major harvest was approved with more than 6,000 deer taken. The first hunt proved the benefits of game management, and an annual lottery system was devised for 2,500 hunting permits. The hunt has become a bonanza for area merchants, and farmers have been able to keep most of their crops.

In 1995, managed hunting of squirrels, turkeys and other small game provided 54,000 hours of sport hunting and another 45,000 hours of sport and commercial fishing. During the summer, 100,000 people used the area for swimming, boating, camping and enjoyment of outdoor life. When the fall migration begins, waterfowl find a choice wintering ground where their privacy is assured.

I was lucky to have hunted and fished in the area before it became a refuge. Bill Clements and I watched hunting change from crop defense to an early bow season; indeed, we took our first archery deer on one of the early bow hunts. The refuge has become an asset to southeastern Arkansas, providing income to local people and a recreation area for families from all over the state.

I heard a man declare that they don't build automobile like they used to. They don't, and I'm glad. The refuge land is not like what it used to be, either, and I'm proud of that. The best change of all is the attitude of local farmers, who say: "The deer herd has been reduced to a level where we can afford to donate a few soybeans to a good cause."

▲

How tax money collected from the manufacturer of sporting goods benefits and promotes the wildlife of this country.

CHAPTER THIRTY-SEVEN

Game Cooking

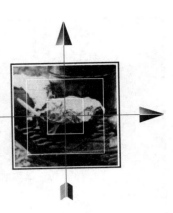

 love the taste of good food, and I enjoy seeking out ways to prepare that food. It's a task that's especially satisfying when I'm preparing the meat of a game animal I've harvested. This chapter is devoted to the cooking of wild game. It includes recipes for cooking your catch and other tips when handling, preparing and serving the meat, all without the services of a professional chef hovering in the background.

Two simple and inexpensive ways to produce a tastier, more enjoyable meal are the use of Kosher salt and the boiling of meat to reduce its fat content. Kosher Salt is a coarse flake salt produced by evaporation or a compaction process for use in Kosher food. The coarse flake crystals surpass ordinary salt in drawing and retaining liquids in the meat-curing process.

Always boil any large or thick cuts of meat prior to the final stage of cooking. You'll be amazed at the amount of fat rising to the water's surface in just 20 minutes of boiling. Carefully pour off the floating fat and cook the meat in the normal manner. Hog, steer, bull or buck will taste much better for it. Removal of the fat will also make your doctor happy and get more compliments for your cooking. Animal fat is generally considered a sign of health and tenderness in animals. The taste of animal fat is at its best when it comes from a hog and served in the form of bacon. Venison fat is animal fat at its worst. Its main function is to keep the deer alive through the winter months. I know a wildlife biologist who swears that bear fat is the best lubrication obtainable for a patched ball in a black powder rifle. This man may shoot bear tallow but he wouldn't eat it if he was starving.

Make a habit of visual examination when field dressing any animal, including squirrel and rabbit. Game-dressing gloves are inexpensive and should be in your hunting kit. These lightweight rubber gloves will protect your hands from a possible infection as well as a messy field dressing chore. A lone tick fleeing from a cooling carcass is easily spotted while crossing a thin white glove. These precautionary steps make good sense and are not meant to scare readers. The possibility remains, though, of contracting Lyme's disease or Rocky Mountain spotted fever when handling unhealthy animals.

An obviously ill game animal should not be field dressed or eaten. If possible, report the sick animal to a wildlife officer. An animal's liver is often a good indicator of its health. Liver fluke is a common disease to wildlife in some areas. This doesn't render the deer unfit

Looking over a portable bar-b-que smoker

for consumption, just the liver. Ask your wildlife officer to identify areas of fluke infestation, remembering that your visual examination is still the final test.

Since wild game has to be collected before it can be cooked, the first recipe in this chapter is suggested for the first night at camp. To motivate your hunting skills, note that not one ingredient comes from wild game. Only one ingredient requires refrigeration and preparation time is fast and easy.

Hunting Camp Stew

(Fills up eight hungry hunters)
- *one lb. coarse ground beef*
- *one medium white onion (chopped)*
- *three or four medium potatoes (chopped)*
- *one No. 2 can of whole kernel corn*
- *one No. 2 can great northern beans*
- *one No. 2 can of pinto or kidney beans*
- *one large can of tomato juice*
- *one tablespoon of chili powder*

Brown and drain the ground beef. Drain the corn and mix with the canned beans. Add the tomato juice and chili powder. Salt lightly; more salt can be added later if desired. Use regular ground black pepper, unless you really want to pep things up (coarse ground black and Louisiana Red applied with caution will stop any accusations of cooking a bland-tasting stew).

✦ *The following recipes will help make your hunting success more enjoyable. Cooking wild meat at 350° is recommended and allows thorough cooking of the meat. Increasing the temperature to 360° is just right for frying fish.*

Smoked Venison Tenders

The ultimate in fine venison — two strips of meat called "the tenders" — lies under the backbone near the pelvic region of deer. Here's how to prepare tenders as part of a delicious meal:

1. Bake two medium-large Idaho potatoes. Coat them with peanut oil and seal them in heavy aluminum foil. Allow about 1 1/2 hours cooking time in a 350° oven, before sprinkling them with Kosher salt.

2. Set up your smoker for a medium-fast smoke, using pecan wood chips as fuel (if available). Allow about 1 1/2 hours to cook the meat all the way through. Baste the two tenders often with peanut oil, and sprinkle on some coarse ground pepper after the first basting. Don't let the meat dry out while cooking. Salt the meat lightly after you remove it from the smoker.

3. When the potatoes are done, open the aluminum foil and sprinkle them again with Kosher salt. Serve them with chives and sour cream.

4. Serve the meat with a cherry sauce and hot rolls. As a side dish, try a green salad with vinegar and oil dressing. A chilled bottle of Arkansas' Wiederkeher's Pink Cataba Wine serves as a fine beverage for this meal.

Smoked Venison Backstrap

A venison backstrap consists of a two-inch thick strip of meat on both sides of the backbone, extending from just behind the animal's shoulders to the top of the hams. As opposed to the tenders, the backstrap is on top of the backbone.

Smoking a thick piece of lean venison requires a degree of skill and experience. The meat can come out too dry if you're inattentive during the process.

1. Prepare a slow smoke fire using pecan wood chips if available. Fat applied to the surface of the meat often fails to permeate, so use a larding needle to inject one or two strips of fresh pork fat or bacon the length of the meat.

2. Fix a baste of equal amounts of hot melted fresh pork fat and Planters peanut oil. Spread the baste with a swab or brush and sprinkle on generously with coarse ground black pepper.

3. Smoke the meat until it is almost done — about three to four hours, depending on your smoker. Inspect the meat frequently and baste it often, so that it won't dry out.

4. Salt the meat lightly just before it is done. Increase the heat; remove the meat as soon as a crust begins to appear.

Do not precut this meat; cut and serve as needed. Smoked backstrap makes a fine main course and can be used for sandwiches the next day when sliced thin and against the grain.

Elaine's Venison Backstrap

Naturally, a host makes every effort to see that his guests are served only the best cuts of chicken and home-cured hams. For generations, host families have called the choice cuts of meat "preacher meat," in reference to the privilege of having the local preacher and his family as guests for dinner after Sunday morning services.

Venison backstrap qualifies as preacher meat. My wife enjoys this cut of meat because of the ease of preparation and its outstanding flavor. Backstraps should be cooked in foil or smoked.

A 12-inch length of backstrap will generally feed four adults. Trim away any white fat

and the silvery muscle sheath. Apply a generous sprinkling of coarse ground black pepper, salt lightly, and crush three bay leaves over the meat. Rub your spices into the meat, then wrap in heavy duty foil and finish in an oven at medium heat. Use a smoker if you prefer.

Serve with broccoli, brussels sprouts or baby green lima beans as a complementary vegetable. Set out French bread toasted with butter and sprinkled with garlic salt. I like Lea and Perrins Sauce and iced tea with this meal.

Elaine's Oven Barbeque

The front shoulders of the animal can either be boned for ground meat, or cooked whole as part of an oven barbecue. The shoulder and the ribs are the only cuts of venison that will cook decently with the bone in them.

1. Wrap the meat in heavy aluminum foil, cooking at 350° until the meat starts to separate from the bone. Drain off the broth, leaving about 2/3 of a cup. Salt the meat lightly and pour a commercial barbecue sauce over it.

2. Put the meat back into the oven for another 35 to 45 minutes. When done, lay the shoulder flat and slice very thin, using an electric knife (if available). This meat also makes good sandwiches.

Clements' Butterfly Steaks

If you stripped the muscle layers from one ham (as mentioned in Chapter 34), the strips can be made into butterfly-shaped steaks. My old bowhunting friend, Bill Clements, passed along the following method for preparing these steaks.

Cooking a meal on a campfire

1. Lay the meat strip flat and make a cut 3/4 of the way through the meat, about 1/2-inch in from the end. Continue making cuts at 1/2-inch intervals all the way through, ending up with a steak an inch thick but cut almost all the way in the center with the two flaps held together at the bottom. Cut more steaks the same way, figuring on three steaks per person.

2. Prepare a batter of 2/3 cup of milk, two eggs, and 2/3 teaspoon of sweet basil.

Pound each steak with a mallet, then drop them in a sack containing flour and coarse ground black pepper. Shake well.

3. Heat the fat in a deep fryer at about 350°. Drop a steak in gently, being careful not to burn the batter. Cook until done, salting lightly as it drains. Check the steak to see if it's to your liking, then adjust cooking time accordingly with the remaining steaks.

Butterfly steaks are a treat on any occasion. They taste great in deer camp where they are fast and easy to prepare. Serve with baked beans, French fries, light bread, sweet purple onion and choice pickles. Very cold sweet milk or hot coffee complements this meal.

Venison Ham In Foil

As with preparing all venison, start by trimming away all white fat and muscle sheath. Apply a generous amount of coarse ground black pepper. Wrap the ham in heavy-duty aluminum foil and cook in a 350° oven for almost five hours. (The bone should have been removed when the deer was dressed, reducing your cooking time.) Drain off the excess broth about halfway through the cooking.

Set up your smoker for a medium-hot smoke. When the ham is done, remove from the oven and sprinkle it lightly with salt. Finish it off in the smoker until a thin crust forms on the meat.

Slice the ham lengthwise (with an electric knife, if possible). Serve the slices on a preheated platter, offering guests a choice of a barbecue sauce or cherry sauce to top it off.

Ground Venison Patties

The neck, forelegs and ribs of deer can be boned for ground meat. Before grinding, all white fat and muscle sheath should be removed. To hold the patties together while cooking, a certain amount of animal fat is needed. Substitute fresh pork or beef.

1. Grind up three pounds of boned venison. Add one pound of lean ground round beef and a pound of ground fresh pork. (This makes a lot of patties; if it's too much for your needs, cut down on the ingredients but with the same proportions.)

2. Add a moderate amount of coarse ground black pepper and salt lightly as you blend the venison, beef and pork. Make the patty about 3/8 inch thick.

I prefer venison hamburgers seared in peanut oil on a hot grill and suggest using a solid iron grill for venison patties.

Serve each patty on a large sesame seed bun and put out plenty of garnishes for individual tastes.

Venison Rib Barbeque

If you saved the ribs instead of boning them out for ground meat, here's how to prepare them as part of a first-class meal:

1. Trim off all visible white fat. Put on a heavy application of coarse ground black pepper. Wrap the ribs in heavy-duty aluminum foil and cook in a 350° oven for approximately three hours.

2. Prepare a hot baste of apple cider vinegar, salt and a dash of French's mustard. While the meat is cooking, prepare a medium-hot charcoal fire mixed with green hickory nuts (complete with hulls, if obtainable). This medium hot fire will remove any remaining white fat residue and improve the flavor of the ribs.

3. Cut the ribs into individual portions. If you have the nerve, serve them with Arkansas City Distillate (see p. TK) as a barbecue sauce. Serve with a salad, French bread with garlic salt, and natural cut french fries. Put out plenty of pickles, olives, garlic butter and sliced sweet onions.

Smoked Venison Jerky

Many people do not think of jerky as uncooked meat, but it is. The meat is cured, rather than cooked. This age-old method of drying and preserving meat involves removing the moisture from the meat. People living in hot, arid climates often let the sun do the drying.

Jerky can be prepared in a smoker using just enough heat to keep the smoke around the meat fairly hot and moisture-free. I like to use pecan or apple wood chips when smoking, which add flavor to the jerky.

1. Start with a marinade, blending one cup of white distilled vinegar, four tablespoons of soy sauce, one tablespoon of coarse ground black pepper and one tablespoon of plain table salt (non-iodized).

2. Using the muscles from the ham, remove all the muscle sheath and white fat. Cut 1/8-inch thick slices lengthwise. Soak the slices in the marinade for four to six hours in your refrigerator, using a glass or ceramic bowl (not metal).

3. Drain the slices, pat them dry with paper towels and let them air dry before putting them in the smoker. (This step reduces the meat's liquid content.) Hang the strips in your smoker for four to six hours.

Test a sample after four hours. The pieces may require more exposure to the smoke, depending on thickness and taste preferences.

Store the jerky in tightly-sealed, moisture-proof fruit jars.

Clements' Wild Turkey Breast

Bill Clements prepares a wild turkey in a different way. The meat comes out delicious and tender when cooked in this fashion.

1. Start with a boned-out turkey breast. Cut the meat into 1/2-inch thick slices and pound them with a mallet. Soak the pieces overnight in butter in the refrigerator.

2. Make a dip using 3/4 cup of milk, two beaten eggs, and 1/2 teaspoon of sweet basil. Stir and blend well. Coat each piece of turkey with the egg dip. Drop the pieces into a paper bag containing flour and shake well.

3. Fry them in medium-hot (350°) grease for about minutes. Test a small piece first; the grease should be hot, but not hot enough to burn the batter.

Remove and drain the slices; salt lightly.

Fried Rattlesnack Backstrap

We often come across a cane brake rattlesnake, which can make an unusual meal. First, of course, shoot the snake through the head. Pin the head to the ground with a stick and cut it off. Bury the head deep. Never touch a poisonous snake's head with your hand or foot; a reflex action could result in a snake bite, even from a severed head.

1. Slit the skin lengthwise along the underside, then peel the skin off. (Be prepared for a reflex action while splitting the skin.) Remove the backstrap from a large rattlesnake by boning each side of the backbone, resulting in two strips of meat as wide and thick as your first two fingers and between two and three feet long.

2. Cut the lengths into three-inch sections. Dip the pieces into a simple milk and egg batter and drop them into a sack holding pepper-seasoned flour. Fry the sections in medium-hot (350°) peanut oil until done in about five minutes.

Arkansas City Distillate

If you like a peppy barbecue sauce with a real kick, try this mixture — it's no sweet, delicate sauce.

1. Blend two tablespoons of salt and sugar into four cups of hot water.

2. Blend four tablespoons each of chili powder and coarse ground black pepper into four cups of apple cider vinegar.

3. Mix the seasoned water and seasoned vinegar together in a one-gallon Pyrex cooker with a lid. Add four cups of ketchup. Stir in one finely-chopped onion.

4. Let the covered mixture simmer outside for three to four hours (a Coleman camp stove is handy for this purpose). Additional salting may be needed near the end of the simmering. ▲

INDEX